KU-346-723

PADDLING BRITAIN

50 BEST PLACES TO EXPLORE BY SUP, KAYAK & CANOE

LIZZIE CARR

Contributing editor
James Lowen

Bradt Travel Guides Ltd, UK
Globe Pequot Press Inc, USA

AUTHOR

Lizzie Carr, aka Lizzie Outside, is a natural-born adventurer, blogger and environmentalist. She has dedicated herself to exploring the length and breadth of Britain on a stand-up paddleboard (SUP), while using her journey to highlight and educate on wider environmental issues affecting our inland waterways and oceans.

In May 2016, Lizzie became the first person in history to paddleboard the length of England's waterways, solo and unsupported. She completed the 400-mile journey in 22 days, taking more than 2,000 photos of plastic pollution she encountered.

A year later, Lizzie completed her next challenge. On 18 May 2017, she became the first woman ever to cross the English Channel alone on a stand-up paddleboard. Lizzie is passionate about championing Britain's waters as rivals to international destinations. *Paddling Britain*, her first book, gives a glimpse of some of her favourite places to explore.

ACKNOWLEDGEMENTS

There are a few very special people who I want to thank for helping me get this book off the ground. First and foremost, thank you to family – Mum, Dad, Angela and David – for your unconditional love and support from the moment I left my job to chase a life more meaningful. Thank you Russell for helping me find the courage to take a leap of faith. Without you, I'm not sure that I would have taken those first steps that have led me here. For that, I am endlessly grateful.

I thank all my friends for rooting for me and keeping me sane, positive and on track both in life and with this book, particularly Clare and Parko – you are both treasures! Thanks to Rich Hounslow for your expertise on all things canoeing. I would also like to say a huge thank you to everyone who has been part of my paddleboarding adventures so far. I am forever thankful for the opportunities I've been granted, the people I've met and the memories I've made along the way. I am very lucky to have so many wonderful people by my side. I also thank Andrew Gilchrist at *the Guardian* for allowing me to reproduce an edited version of my article in that newspaper.

Finally, a big thank you to the wonderful team that has helped me get this book published: Jennifer, Anna, Rachel and, of course, the invaluable input from my editor James, without whom I couldn't have done this.

CONTENTS

↑ Kayaking on the River Dee (page 156). (SS)

INTRODUCTION

Four years ago I was sitting behind my desk at work. Not only had I never tried paddleboarding, but I don't think I even knew what a 'paddleboard' was. If you had told me then that, by 2018, I would have completed two world firsts on a paddleboard, launched a nationwide campaign to rid our planet of plastic pollution and written a guide to paddling and its sister waterborne activities of kayaking and canoeing, I would have retorted that you were insane. Yet a pastime that I took up by accident just three years ago has completely transformed my existence. I am penning this book in the hope that it will similarly enhance your life.

As many people who have tried paddling, canoeing or kayaking will know, it is surprisingly easy to get hooked the moment you first dip your paddle into the water and take your inaugural stroke. For many of us, there is no looking back. Everything feels right: physical benefits (low-impact exercise and a full-body workout) combined with insurmountable benefits to wellbeing (being outside, in nature, at one with the elements – and exploring our world from a different perspective).

Some may find paddleboarding, kayaking or canoeing to be repetitive and, at times, monotonous – especially on long journeys. But, for many of us, that routine is part of the charm. Developing a regular rhythm can transport you into your own realm, safe from the pressures and stresses of everyday life, and protected from incidental distractions. On days when it's literally just the water and you, it is easier to feel deeply – gently, mindfully – connected to the elements.

Over the last couple of years I have spent a lot of time exploring Britain on my paddleboard. I have relished the opportunity to rediscover the beauty of the country in entirely new ways and find new meaning in what I observe and experience. Through this book, I encourage you to do the same. Whether you use a board, canoe or kayak, paddle without rushing. Take time out to watch the world go by. Use paddling as a counterpoint to an ever-speedier life. On a paddleboard, canoe or kayak, absolutely do not beast through countryside, racing past farms, fells and wildlife trying to reach the finish line. Instead, I am immersed in nature, becoming part of it for a brief time. I hope the same is – or will be – true for you.

But where best to experience the richness that paddling offers? People often ask where I recommend for paddling or which waterways I like the most. This guide enables me to share my favourites, and to encourage you to explore British waterways, to paddle Britain. Together we can breathe life into our canals, rivers and coast – revealing new places to explore and offering fresh perspectives on our beautiful island.

My selection is intentionally varied. Some routes are picturesque, others less so. Some chosen waterways are full of wildlife, others industrial or urban. There are

→ Lizzie out on Plastic Patrol. (Andy Hargraves)

canals and rivers, but also lochs and coasts. Itineraries stretch from the Isles of Scilly (in southwest England) to the historic county of Sutherland (in northern Scotland). They cover secluded retreats in addition to well-known sites, and historic locations alongside paddles through stunning countryside. There are journeys short and long, considerately marshalled routes and excursions where you are freer to follow your whim. As a collection, my suggestions are intended to reflect the breadth and diversity of Britain's waterways. Wherever you live, or wherever you wish to travel, there should be a route to entice you on to the water, paddle in hand.

I hope that your explorations will leave you with as many treasured memories as they have me. I still smile at my father's delighted reaction – off a beach on Scilly – at me managing to balance on a paddleboard for the very first time. Then there's the route I suggest for the Lancaster Canal (page 180), which is imbued with personal significance as it formed the final 20 miles of my seminal 400-mile paddle through England. Beneath bright blue skies and golden sunshine, and despite being both exhausted and filthy, I completed my goal on a tranquil, disused canal – and was rewarded with one of the most spectacular sunsets I have ever witnessed from the water.

Our waterways get a bit of a hard time yet they have provided me with both access to a sport I love and the setting for great adventures. I hope they furnish you with as much happiness as they have me. After all, our rivers and canals need us. Collectively we can re-energise these escapes. Together we can appreciate their history, meaning and rich wildlife. Joining forces, we can address environmental blights such as plastic pollution – a truly modern-day curse. Our waterways – canals, rivers and the sea – are our aquatic playground. Provided we care for them, they will continue to be so for future generations as well. Britain's waters have been there for me when I've needed peace, calm and perspective. As a result I feel very protective of them – and I bet you do too. Let's celebrate, enjoy, protect and cherish our blue planet.

PADDLING: THE ESSENTIALS

You can approach the routes suggested in this book on a stand-up paddleboard (usually known by its acronym of SUP), canoe or kayak. I have come to love the former, but the other two activities may grab you more keenly. Much of my advice is common to all three ways to experience the water – but there are also specific differences worth noting.

The rise of affordable and easily transportable entry-level equipment – notably boards, including inflatable ones, and paddles – has democratised waterborne activities such as paddling. Many watersport enthusiasts are skilled and knowledgeable and understand full well the importance of carrying the relevant safety equipment and checking conditions. The following words are a reminder of what they already know. For people trying the activity for the first time or with little prior experience or appreciation of how conditions affect paddling, reading the following sections are a must – although, for the avoidance of doubt, not a substitute for a proper lesson from a qualified instructor. So whether you are planning a casual paddle around a harbour or are opting for a longer coastal trek around a rugged coastline, read on for the key considerations and top tips that all paddlers, kayakers and canoeists should follow.

STAND-UP PADDLEBOARDING

Choose the correct length of paddle   Make sure your paddle is the right length. I do this by putting the blade on the ground, holding the paddle vertically by my side, and extending my hand above my head with a slight bend in my elbow. Your wrist should be able to rest on what is called the T-grip (the 'T'-shaped handle at the top of the paddle), with your hand dropping over the other side. If you are straining to reach the T-grip, the paddle is too long for you.

Stand up tall   Posture is important, both for efficient paddling and to minimise the stress on your body. Stand tall with your feet shoulder-width apart. Place one hand on the T-grip at the top of the paddle and the other on the shaft at a point marginally wider than the distance between your feet. Look straight

↑ Standing tall (Andy Hargraves)

ahead and bend your knees slightly – the flex will help you stay stable on the board. If you are having problems standing up then kneel down for a while to get a feel for the board before trying to stand. One tip for standing is to get some momentum by paddling, as the forward movement helps keep the board stable.

Stroke skills The key to good technique is to 'stack' your arms along the paddle. This means keeping your top hand (which is on the T-grip) and bottom hand (which holds the shaft) perpendicular to one another as you enter the water. Then draw back alongside the board. Finish the stroke at your ankles; resist the temptation to draw back further as this creates drag that will accelerate fatigue. Use your core to propel yourself; your arms are there to grip the paddle but the majority of power could be coming from your glutes and abdominal muscles.

Changing direction It's important to master board control before taking on more challenging paddles. There are some simple core techniques to practise to get you started. First, place the paddle in the water and push water towards the tail of the board on one side and the nose on the other – making a wider circular motion around the board. Turning the face of the blade away will help you turn more swiftly. Second, get to grips with a stroke called the 'Big C'. Push the paddle into the water at the front of the board and arc a wide 'C' around the board until you bring the paddle in behind you. This is another stroke that enables you to turn the board quickly if you need to alter direction.

CANOEING & KAYAKING

By Richard Hounslow (double Olympic silver medallist in the Canoe Slalom)

This advice is very much the basics. I strongly recommend that you visit the British Canoeing website (⊘ tinyurl.com/start-canoeing) to find out more about getting started and to brief yourself on aspects ranging from equipment to types of canoeing.

For kayaking, you use a double-ended paddle that is suitable whether you are right- or left-handed. Posture is important. Sit up straight, with a slight bend forward at the hips. As you paddle, reach forward with a slightly bent elbow. Pull the blade towards your hips and rotate for maximum power and efficiency. Repeat this motion on the opposite side, building up into an efficient paddling rhythm.

For canoeing, it is best to use a single-bladed paddle with a 'T-grip'. This is similar to the paddle used for stand-up paddleboarding, but shorter. Again, posture is key. Sit up straight, reaching forward with a slightly bent elbow and flexing forward at the hips. Pull the blade towards your hips then sit up straight. Repeat to gain momentum. Steering involves switching the side that you paddle or using a 'cross bow stroke', where you reach across the bow (front) of the canoe.

There are several basic turning strokes that are useful for both kayaking and canoeing. Here are three:

Sweep   Reach forward with your stroke and 'sweep' towards the stern (back of the boat) in a wide arc. This moves the boat away from the stroke.

Bow rudder   Slice the blade forward, opening out its face as you do so. This draws the boat towards the stroke.

Reverse   Place the blade in the water then, using the back of the blade, move it towards the bow (front) of the boat in a wide arc. This also moves the boat towards the stroke.

PADDLING SAFELY

All watersports come with risk; paddling, canoeing and kayaking are no different. Whether your route encompasses flat water or surf, there are things you can look out for or actions you can take to ensure your safety. Paddling safely is your responsibility; take it seriously and heed the advice below.

PARTNER UP

Paddling (or canoeing or kayaking) with a partner is an important component of safety – but comes with a whole heap of other benefits too (companionship,

WILD CAMPING ETIQUETTE

Phoebe Smith, wild-camping adventurer and author of Wilderness Weekends

One of the most common questions I am asked about wild camping is: 'am I really allowed to do it?'. When it comes to suggested spots, wild camping is only officially permitted in Scotland and on Dartmoor. Elsewhere, you are supposed to ask the landowner's permission first. From experience, however, this is usually either impractical or impossible. Generally though, it's all a case of etiquette. The following guidelines should help:

A WILD SLEEPER'S ETIQUETTE

- Arrive late; leave early.
- Sleep well above the wall line, away from people's houses.
- Leave no trace of your camp (take all rubbish with you).
- Save fires for the bothies; don't light them in the great outdoors and risk damaging fragile ecosystems.
- Bury your toilet waste and pack out all paper and sanitary products.
- Be respectful at all times. If asked to move on, do so.
- Always aim to leave a wild place – whether camp spot, cave, beach or bothy – in a better condition than when you found it.
- Always close gates behind you.
- If you take a dog with you, keep it on a lead around livestock or where signs indicate that you should.

fun, cost-sharing etc). That said, there are times when getting out on the water alone is also important. In such instances, make sure you let someone know your itinerary (see *Tell a friend*, page 14).

LEASH UP

Given that the board is your most buoyant piece of equipment, staying with it is important. If you fall into fast-moving or tidal water, it is easy to be separated from your board. In most circumstances, my advice (particularly directed at beginners) is to wear a leash, even in still water.

WEAR A BUOYANCY AID

A Personal Flotation Device (PFD) not only keeps you safe but also warm. There are a whole host of different type of buoyancy aids available – from life jackets like those found on tourist boats to waistbands that you pull a cord to inflate. It is important to consider the level of buoyancy required to keep you afloat should you fall in the water; ensure that your PFD is adequate for the circumstances you will encounter. Personally, I like ones with pockets, as these are helpful for safeguarding phone, keys, energy bars etc. Ensure that your PFD fits correctly and that all straps are securely fastened. If crotch straps are fitted, use these too.

PADDLEBOARDING & ME

Adapted from an article I wrote for the Guardian, 1 October 2016, *and reproduced with that newspaper's kind permission.*

In May 2016, I travelled nearly 650km (400 miles) on my paddleboard, covering the length of England in 22 days, and carrying everything I needed – 20kg of kit – on my board. I'd do 30km (20 miles) a day, wild camping and waking up to beautiful views of the waterways of England, the stunning canals and rivers that carried me from Surrey to Cumbria, passing kingfishers, herons, hedgehogs and swans on the way.

I'd trained hard, but paddling 11 hours a day was exhausting. I travelled north on the advice of a friend, who thought that the prevailing winds would help, but I ended up with gusts in my face 90% of the way. This also meant travelling upstream along (against!) the Thames. At the start, heavy rain and high winds made this incredibly difficult. You can't simply stop in the middle of a river when you're going against the current. It took a week of relentless paddling just to get past the Thames section and into the Oxford Canal.

By day 15, I couldn't clench my fists. This was the start of carpal tunnel syndrome (where a nerve in the wrist is compressed, painfully). Some days it took hours for me to grip properly: my hands were like pincers as I tried to pull on my leggings each morning. The worst point was the appropriately named Heartbreak Hill. This stretch of the Trent and Mersey Canal has 29 locks, which I had to pass in a single

KNOW THE WEATHER & TIDES

Before departing on any paddle, it is essential to check the weather and (where relevant) tides and water levels as well. Wind strength and direction are key; particularly be aware of winds blowing you further offshore. If you have a smartphone, there are a number of apps (with sister websites) that you can check in advance (and during your paddle!) to get a steer on conditions and tides. I suggest looking at all three of the following and coming to a considered judgement on current conditions before setting off: Magic Seaweed (good for surf and swell); Met Office (general weather conditions); and Wind Guru (wind direction, gusts and speed).

For tides, I recommend the Tides Planner app. If you do not have a smartphone, but do have access to a computer, check tide times on ⊘ metoffice.gov.uk/public/weather/tide-times/.

BE HUMBLE

Never forget that water is untamable and potentially powerful. Be cautious about your abilities and never underestimate the rate at which weather and water conditions can change. Respect the water at all times. It is mightier than you can ever be.

day – hauling my board and equipment on and off the water every time. By lock six, I was sobbing. I felt tired, hungry, alone. But I wasn't going to give up.

Why did I put myself through this? Well, I'd always been adventurous, but I found myself stuck in the corporate world, working in marketing. I was ambitious and defined success by job titles and pay. After five years, I decided to take a career break – to explore the world before knuckling back down.

Suddenly I was young and free again. I had incredible adventures: trekking in China, horseriding in Outer Mongolia. It reignited my love for the outdoors and made me feel invincible. But three months after I returned to work, I was diagnosed with thyroid cancer. This blindsided me. My thyroid was removed and I had radiotherapy. I went to stay with my dad on the Isles of Scilly, to relax and recover. I was struggling with fatigue so high-impact exercise was now out of the question.

One day as I sat on the beach, I saw someone paddleboarding. It looked so relaxing. I walked straight to the sailing club and borrowed a board. Although I fell into the water a bit, paddleboarding proved easy to pick up. That's the beauty of this activity – anyone can do it. And it's very safe: if you can't see the bottom of the sea, they say, you're too far out. It's not 'trendy punting', as sceptics bluster – it's Britain's fastest growing watersport for a good reason. People fall in love with it because, mentally and physically, it feels so beneficial, so calming.

One of the best paddleboarding tips is to keep moving forward as soon as you're standing. That way, the board's more stable, easier to control. Paddle, don't idle. It's good advice for life.

FUEL UP & KEEP HYDRATED

Paddling can burn up to 400 calories an hour. Particularly if you're doing long paddles, bring food such as energy bars. As a low-impact sport it's easy to think you're not working up much of a sweat, but believe me – you do. So keep watered. If you're doing an endurance paddle, consider adding some electrolytes (as are often contained in sports drinks).

TELL A FRIEND

Tell someone back on land where you are going and what time you anticipate getting back. If you're going coastal, also advise the local coastguard of your plans or, better still, sign up to the HM Coastguard's Voluntary Safety Identification Scheme (⊘ mcanet.mcga.gov.uk/public/cg66/). You should also carry a suitable means of calling for help. In most cases, this will be an adequately charged mobile phone, ideally carried in a waterproof case or dry bag. In an area of little reception, take a VHF radio as well.

AVOIDING WATERBORNE ILLNESSES

Be aware of waterborne diseases when paddling on channels and inland waterways. Current widespread problems include blue-green algae and Weil's disease. Before you eat, either wash your hands in clean water or use hand sanitiser. Wash your kit thoroughly after use.

WHAT TO WEAR

In warmer months, when temperatures have increased, loose, breathable clothing (not jeans!) is fine, but cooler or windier weather (and thus damper conditions) will likely make a wetsuit preferable. Suitable footwear includes old trainers or sports sandals. That said, I sometimes like to paddle in neoprene boots or barefoot. A hat is important, whether a cap (summer) or warm, woolly hat (winter). If you are paddling on white water wearing a helmet is always recommended.

ADVENTURE KIT LIST

If you're planning a paddle adventure – and what constitutes an 'adventure' partly depends on your level of experience – there are some key considerations to (literally!) take on board. Paddleboards usually have lashings towards the front, to which you can secure dry bags. Canoes and kayaks make things easier with dedicated storage space. While varying from the seemingly obvious to the somewhat peculiar, items on my suggested kit list have all saved me both time and trouble at some point on my adventures. Key are: gloves (in cold weather); dry bag or bags; refillable water bottle with purification filter (but only use with fresh water); maps (I use Ordnance Survey digital maps); suncream; spare clothes; and

a waterproof phone case (or a waterproof phone). If you are travelling beyond sheltered waters then I also suggest taking four waterproof items: compass; watch; GPS; and torch (plus working batteries).

PADDLING RESPONSIBLY

As paddlers, canoeists or kayakers, it is important that we paddle responsibly. This takes several forms.

JOIN #PLASTICPATROL

In 2016 I started Plastic Patrol (⊘ plasticpatrol.co.uk), a nationwide campaign to rid Britain's waterways of rubbish. The aim is not only to help restore our rivers and canals back to their original beauty so that we can better enjoy them but to also intercept the 80% of plastic that emanates from inland locations yet ends up in our oceans. Once plastic hits the ocean, 99% of it sinks – lost in a blue abyss and left to fragment over hundreds of years creating all sorts of problems. You might think I am simply motivated by making my playground a more appealing place to paddle. But that is largely a side benefit. The bigger, indeed catastrophic, issue at play is that plastic is killing our marine life. I for one cannot stand by and watch while our species has such a detrimental impact on aquatic and marine ecosystems.

↑ Stay connected to your paddleboard by leashing it to your leg (page 12). (Lizzie Carr)

The chances are that, having bought this book, you are a water lover and paddler – just like me. If so, I ask you to join me in the fight against plastic pollution. Doing this is straightforward. Download the Plastic Patrol app (available on the App Store) and, when you hit the water, please take a moment to collect rubbish that you see and log it on the app. Every little piece removed helps. Or join a clean-up event organised by #PlasticPatrol. On boards we can access parts of waterways that are inaccessible by foot or other means. So let's do something positive about it. Let's be responsible paddlers. Let's all be part of #PlasticPatrol.

RESPECT AQUATIC WILDLIFE

Paddling responsibly also means being aware of seasons and what this means for aquatic wildlife. There are some routes that include paddles past protected areas or islands to which access is forbidden at some times of the year (eg: the breeding season for birds). Please ensure that you check and adhere to these restrictions. Additionally, please respect individual animals: allow seals and the like to approach you rather than chasing after them.

MINIMISE THREATS FROM NON-NATIVE WILDLIFE

Another important issue affecting Britain's rivers and lakes is the spread of non-native species of plants and animals. 'Invasive alien species' (as they are often known) are having a detrimental impact on indigenous British species and

↑ Lizzie primed and ready for Plastic Patrol. (Andy Hargraves)

PADDLING THROUGH ENGLAND'S PLASTIC

Adapted from an article I wrote for the Guardian, *1 October 2016, and reproduced with that newspaper's kind permission.*

It was seeing a coot's nest constructed as much from plastic as from vegetation that galvanised me into action. I resolved to draw attention to what was happening on our watery doorstep. This prompted my decision to paddleboard the length of England, along its connected waterways, photographing every piece of plastic I saw, geo-tagging the location to create an online map that showed the scale of the problem. Although rubbish increased around towns and cities, even remote areas had plastic bags lurking in trees or bottles in the water. I was horrified.

To up the ante, I then revisited the four worst-affected spots to collect all the rubbish I saw. I spent 7 hours on the banks of the River Trent, gathering 1,000 or so bottles into a 'trash raft' that I then paddled along the river. The people I passed were always shocked to find out where the trash came from. I hope that what they learnt has changed their behaviour. As you paddle through Britain, and remove the plastic you encounter, take a moment to tell passers-by what you are doing and why. Together, we can improve Britain's waterways.

ecosystems. Sometimes their presence can be so disruptive that they can alter the entire ecology of a waterbody. Paddlers can unwittingly transfer animals, eggs, larvae and plant fragments between waterbodies via their clothing and equipment. Accordingly, please follow the Check–Clean–Dry biosecurity procedure (*⊘* nonnativespecies.org/checkcleandry/) to help prevent such movement.

If facilities allow, hose down all equipment and clothing, ideally avoiding any watercourses or drainage system. Clothing and equipment should be allowed to dry for 48 hours before being used elsewhere.

GET LICENSED

Organisations such as the Canal and River Trust (which is responsible for managing and safeguarding more than 3,000km/2,000 miles of waterways in England and Wales; *⊘* canalrivertrust.org.uk) and Scottish Canals (responsible for Scottish canals; *⊘* scottishcanals.co.uk) require you to have a licence for paddling on their estate. Please ensure you have one before taking to the water.

You can purchase an annual licence as part of membership of the British Canoeing (*⊘* britishcanoeing.org.uk), or seek a specific licence for waterways managed by the Canal and River Trust, the Environment Agency (*⊘* tinyurl.com/e-agency) or – in the Norfolk Broads – the Broads Authority (*⊘* broads-authority.gov.uk). Please also check whether local permissions are needed for a particular waterway, as they are on the River Beaulieu paddle in this book, for example (see *Titbits*, page 79).

USING THIS GUIDE

In this book, I suggest 50 cracking waterborne itineraries that will serve you equally well whether you are a paddler, canoeist or kayaker. Collectively, the routes suggested will suit different levels of experience – from the casual paddler to the more experienced watersports adventurer. Each route has been selected for its scenic, cultural, historical or wildlife interest – or, more often than not, for a mixture of these reasons. Each paddle I outline has inspired or excited me. I hope it will do the same for you too.

Each chapter starts with the headlines of the paddle in question. The waterway or location and county are specified. I indicate the launch point (complete with a grid reference) and identify the end point where this differs from the launch (which it is not for round trips or there-and-back paddles). Then follows the 'vital statistics' for the paddle, namely: ↔ distance; ⌛ likely duration where this exceeds one day (but not otherwise, as an individual's rate of progress depends on their speed and stamina as well as the conditions and mode of transport chosen); and ① grade. The last equates to the level of difficulty of the paddle; see *How hard is the route?* below for details.

Formalities over, I offer my take on what is particularly exciting about the route. I want to inspire you to travel to the starting point and prepare to launch. I follow this with a detailed description of the route, headed *Paddle this way*. This explains where you start and finish, and guides you along the waterway between points of interest. Follow this in conjunction with a suitable map (and perhaps a smartphone GPS app) and you shouldn't get lost.

HOW HARD IS THE ROUTE?

Each route in this book has been allocated a grade based on the following system, which applies solely to SUP (ie: not to canoeing or kayaking):

① Easily paddled by beginners. It consists of non-tidal and largely sheltered routes.
② Good for amateurs looking to improve their skills on the water. Some consideration around tides and weather conditions are needed.
③ Suitable routes for experienced paddlers, plus novices wanting more of a challenge. These routes require some knowledge and understanding of tides and weather conditions.
④ For intermediate to more advanced paddlers who are competent and experienced in tidal waters.
⑤ Not for the faint-hearted. Only attempt these challenging routes if you significant skills, knowledge and experience. Examples include long coastal paddles with little chance to 'escape' once you have committed, to fast-flowing white waters that demand considerable strength, agility and nous.

FEEDBACK REQUEST

Have you been inspired to paddle one of Lizzie's recommended routes? Or want to suggest one that you feel should have been included? Or fancy sending an update about conditions on the route? Why not write and tell us about your experiences using this guide? You can send your feedback to us on ☏ 01753 893444 or ✉ info@bradtguides.com. We will forward emails to Lizzie who may post updates on the Bradt website at ⬦ bradtupdates.com/paddling. Alternatively you can add a review of the book to ⬦ bradtguides.com or Amazon. Please also communicate your adventures on Twitter, Instagram, Facebook and YouTube using the hashtag #PaddlingBritain and we'll share it for you.

🇫 Bradt Travel Guides & lizzieoutside   🅿 bradtguides & lizzieoutside

🐦 @BradtGuides & @LizzieOutside   ▶ bradtguides & lizzieoutside

📷 @bradtguides & @lizzie_outside

I then follow this with a section on practicalities. *Getting there* summarises access to the launch point by private transport and, wherever possible, by public transport too. All my paddleboards are inflatable, which means that they can be folded neatly down into small rucksacks and easily transported on trains and buses. For anyone using a hard board (of any kind), this is generally impractical so worth bearing in mind when choosing which routes to try (or how to travel there).

Not all of us want to travel encumbered with equipment or feel happy venturing into new waters without expert help. Accordingly, a section on *Hire & lessons* suggests a local provider who can rent you stuff, give lessons or offer guided tours.

I then offer a couple of proposals for *Where to stay & eat*. On occasion, this also includes suggestions for wild camping (ie: not a dedicated campsite), for which read explorer and Bradt author Phoebe Smith's advice on page 11.

In Britain's temperate climate, the default is to paddle during summer – but, in some locations, there are good reasons why you might take to the water in other seasons. If this is the case, I make my view clear in *When to go*.

Finally, in many chapters, I also include a section called *Titbits*. This is where I brigade relevant information that does not fit elsewhere – anything from idiosyncrasies of the route to particular advice or warnings about the difficulty of the paddle. If this section features in a particular chapter, please ensure you read all of it to avoid missing something critical.

There are some chapters where I suggest taking your board to shore and exploring a particular feature by foot. Please use common sense and discretion before leaving your equipment. Be sure to take valuables (and perhaps even your paddle) with you. If you are on a tidal route, you should also consider how this might affect where you leave the board. You don't want to return and find that the rising tide has washed your board offshore.

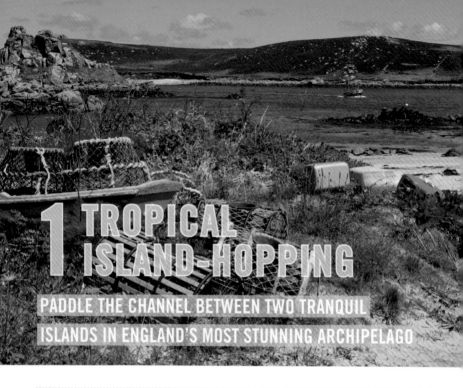

1 TROPICAL ISLAND-HOPPING

PADDLE THE CHANNEL BETWEEN TWO TRANQUIL ISLANDS IN ENGLAND'S MOST STUNNING ARCHIPELAGO

WHERE	Isles of Scilly, Cornwall
STATS	←→ 6.5km (4 miles) round trip ③
START/FINISH	Green Bay, Bryher ♀ SV879146

Life on the Isles of Scilly (alternatively known as 'the Scillies' and pronounced 'silly') revolves around water, which is unsurprising given that it comprises five inhabited islands (the largest, St Mary's, being barely three miles long) and around 130 small rocky islets. The archipelago is situated 45km (28 miles) off Cornwall's Land's End. Partly thanks to its position cosseted by the Gulf Stream, a current of mild water originating in the Gulf of Mexico and flowing eastwards across the Atlantic to northwest Europe, Scilly is blessed with warm climates, sandy beaches, turquoise seas, and wildlife in abundance. It's a little piece of the Caribbean... in England. I kid you not! The subtropical vibe is precisely what you can expect as you paddle in the sheltered Tresco channel that separates two of the inhabited islands in the northwest of the group, namely Bryher and Tresco.

The Isles of Scilly are one of the finest places in Britain to explore from the water. In recent years this once little-known gem has evolved into a Mecca for aquatic-adventure lovers. People travel from all over the world to snorkel, swim and paddle around its magnificent shoreline. The Isles of Scilly has played host to a series of international open-water swimming events, and is well known for its weekly gig-racing. Diving is also popular: there are more than 500 registered shipwrecks scattered around the archipelago.

↑ Life on the island of Bryher, indeed on Scilly more widely, revolves around the sea. (SS)

All this watery excitement and we haven't even covered the wildlife that you might spot… The Isles of Scilly is home to everything from puffins and Atlantic grey seals to rare species of migrating birds that pass through seasonally. As well as puffins, breeding seabirds include shags and guillemots. Take a boat trip offshore and there's a chance of bumping into a basking shark or a pod of short-beaked common dolphins. On land there are creatures found nowhere else in Britain such as 'Scilly bees' (technically a subspecies of moss carder-bee) and 'Scilly shrews' (formally known as lesser white-toothed shrew). There are even prickly stick-insects, which arrived with imported plants but are now embedded here. With a whole heap of wildlife to enjoy you'd be (if you can forgive me the pun) silly not to take a pair of binoculars with you.

PADDLE THIS WAY

Bryher has been described as the 'island of contrasts' given its remarkably varied coastline. The force of the Atlantic Ocean constantly pounds the western side while the eastern edge where the launch point of Green Bay is situated, is exposed to calmer waters. Before you jump aboard, stop for a moment and look directly around. Remains from a floating dock, once based at the Royal Navy flying boat station on Tresco during World War I, can be seen among rocks on the beach. Looking directly ahead (east), beyond the smooth sheet of blue sea, is the low-lying island of Tresco – fundamentally green but lined with pink sea thrift. The

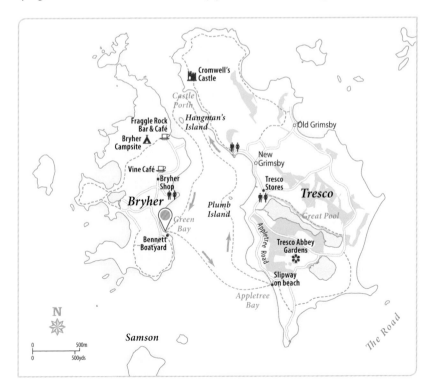

island is widely revered for its beautiful landscape, notably its world-renowned exotic gardens created in the late 1800s when Tresco was little more than a lawless backwater of Britain and its rich history, myth and legend – some believe the island is the final resting place of King Arthur – that define this otherwise innocuous but inhabited rock.

Begin your paddle among the anchored boats bobbing around the small, sandy bay. As you leave the shelter of Green Bay, continue south following Bryher's coastline. You may feel the wind pick up a little as you enter waters that are more exposed to the Atlantic Ocean. You will soon notice the southern tip of the island disappear, which is unsurprising given that the island is less than 1.5km (1 mile) from end to end. Beyond (to the south) is the uninhabited island of Samson.

Begin the 700m (½ mile) paddle eastsoutheast across to Tresco. (The precise distance will depend on where the state of the tide lets you paddle.) At its narrowest point (further north than your crossing point), the channel separating Tresco from Bryher is just 220m wide; on extreme spring tides, you can walk across! Look out for a long, sandy strand becoming ever more prominent. This is Appletree Bay, Tresco's southernmost beach. Pull ashore and sink your toes into the shimmering white sand, looking roughly west across a blue expanse that stretches unabated to the horizon. The next landmass is North America, some 3,000km (1,865 miles) away. This is a paddle right at the edge of Britain.

Tresco, the second largest of the Scillies, is privately owned. If you fancy exploring on land, there's much to see including Bronze Age burial sites and freshwater pools. If you wander up the pathway that leads east from the northeast corner of the beach, you reach Appletree Road, which you can follow east for 500m (⅓ mile) to reach the famous Tresco Abbey Gardens. This horticulturalist's paradise is home to some 20,000 exotic plants from far-flung corners of the globe.

Back on the water, paddle briefly west then head north, hugging Tresco's western shoreline as the island starts to run broadly parallel with Bryher again. You'll pass a rocky outcrop (rather grandiosely called Plumb Island). At low tide you'll need to give this a wide berth, by dog-legging west then east. A mere 500m (⅓ mile) further north, at the other end of the bay, is New Grimsby Quay, home to an inconspicuous shop selling delicious Cornish ice cream in a range of flavours. (I can vouch for the salted caramel scoop – made with Cornish sea salt, no less. Indulge; you've earned it.)

Back aboard, continue northwest, parallel with Tresco's shoreline. Another 1km (⅝ mile) north you reach an enclosed bay named Castle Porth that gives access to Cromwell's Castle, a coastal artillery fort designed to prevent enemy naval ships entering the harbour at New Grimsby.

For an unassuming island, Tresco has a rather unruly past. It has been part of the front line of Britain's defences since the 16th century, and this disused fort,

built in 1651–52 and occupied by Royalists during the English Civil War, is a nod to the significant role the island played. It is open to the public if you fancy exploring it. Haul your board out of the water, then climb the rocks and follow the manmade indentations up a steep verge to wind up just behind it, before making your way to the castle's entrance. It is even well worth the short climb just to enjoy the views from the circular gun tower. From Cromwell's Castle, finish the route by traversing across the channel southwest, back towards Bryher – a much narrower crossing compared with that between Bryher and Appletree Bay. Then head south again towards Green Bay.

Finally, here are a couple of ideas to lend an extra dimension to an already glorious paddle. First, prompted by the number of lobster pots that you will spot en route, why not try fishing from your board? After all, Scilly is a well-known spot for mackerel and pollock: you just need a bit of patience. Second, don't forget to look down. In the shallows, the water is so clear you'll be able to see fish swimming. Third, look out for Hangman Island that sits in Tresco channel, named for the apparent role it played as an execution point by Admiral Blake in the Civil War. There's nothing more to do than paddle up and sit and marvel at the vistas that surround you. But – particularly after an adventurous day's paddling – isn't that simply a beautiful thing to do? When you've had your fill of lolling, paddle the short way back to Green Bay, where you finish.

↑ Land on Tresco to explore Cromwell's Castle. (Russell Howard)

Short-beaked common dolphins are often seen around the Isles of Scilly. Keep an eye out on *Paddles 1* and *2*. (SS)

GETTING THERE

Travel to the Isles of Scilly (⌂ visitislesofscilly.com) is by sea from Penzance (c 2¾ hours) or by air from Exeter, Bristol, Penzance or Newquay (⌂ islesofscilly-travel.co.uk). If you are taking your own equipment, beware of weight restrictions. All routes from the mainland arrive on the island of St Mary's, from where boats depart for other islands (⌂ scillyboating.co.uk).

HIRE & LESSONS

Bennett Boatyard on Bryher (⌂ bennettboatyard.com) offers kayak and board hire and can drop off to other islands if booked in advance.

WHERE TO STAY & EAT

Bryher Campsite (⌂ bryhercampsite.co.uk) is a short walk to the shore. It has excellent amenities and facilities (even renting bell tents to those who prefer to travel light) and its position on a small hill offers lovely views over the bays. Further accommodation options are at ⌂ bryher-islesofscilly.co.uk. The superbly named Fraggle Rock Bar and Café (⌂ bryher. co/fraggle-rock) is right next to the campsite, while a short walk south brings you to Vine Café and Bryher Shop (⌂ bryhershop.co.uk), where you can buy supplies and pick up a piece of traditional 'tattie cake'.

TITBITS

Note that the waters around Cromwell Castle, and north of there (ie: off route), are known to be deep and can get quite choppy.

2 SIMPLY BEACHY

TAKE TO THE WATER FOR A VOYAGE OF DISCOVERY TO SCILLY'S REMOTE EASTERN ISLES

WHERE	Isles of Scilly, Cornwall
STATS	←→ 6km (3¾ miles) one-way or 9km (6 miles) round trip including the Eastern Isles ③
START/FINISH	Old Grimsby Quay, Tresco ♀ SV894156

In the Isles of Scilly, nature is key. Cars are largely unseen on some islands – often replaced with golf buggies. Instead, there are miles of unspoilt beaches, often with a striking and enticing curve of pale sand that shelves into sea with glimmering hues of blue and green. Paddling adventures in these parts are serene events, where breathtaking scenery and tranquillity are characteristic.

St Martin's is one of the smaller inhabited islands in the Scilly archipelago, with a population numbering around 140. It also lays claim to not only the area's best beaches but some of the finest in Britain. The coastlines of St Martin's can boast white sand, azure waters and a real sense of isolation. Have a bathe, share a picnic and indulge in its magnificence before heading to Scilly's Eastern Isles... In my opinion, this makes for one of Britain's most stunning coastal paddles.

The Eastern Isles are a group of 12 small islands that form a Site of Special Scientific Interest (SSSI). The islands are uninhabited but that's not to say they are bereft of life. Many types of mammal and animal flourish here, making for a particularly rewarding paddle. You should anticipate finding rabbits (visible on shore while you paddle around the islands), Atlantic grey seal and several species of seabird with nationally important populations. Try your hand at differentiating cormorant from shag (a tip: look for the former's white cheek patch and the latter's curly crest). Puffin and Manx shearwater are not likely to cause identification mishaps, but both are species renowned for living in one of the few breeding colonies in England. Just don't expect to see any people.

↑ The beach at Old Grimsby on Tresco, where you launch for this paddle. (James LePage/S)

PADDLE THIS WAY

While one side of Tresco runs parallel with Bryher (two islands connected by a route presented on page 20), its other (eastern) flank faces the island of St Martin's and a small, uninhabited islet called Tean. The latter consists of a sprinkling of sandy bays that, at low tide, connect by land to offshore rocks and cairns. Take your pick of starting point on Tresco – either Old Grimsby Quay or one of the wide, sandy beaches that flank it (Raven Port to the north or Green Porth to the south).

Then, paddle towards the smaller island of St Martin's, looping northeast through a small cluster of islands. Just west of St Martin's, you reach Tean. Stop off on the inviting shores of East Porth (the easternmost beach on the islet's southern shore) and explore.

Although its neighbours (Round Island and St Helen's) are susceptible to big rolling swells, Tean is largely protected from the North Atlantic winds. It is also flanked by the smaller – and odd-sounding – islets of Old Man, Crump Island and Pednbrose. While St Helen's can boast the remains of an early Christian chapel, Tean has its own distinct appeal. It is designated as an SSSI; carefully controlled grazing has allowed tiny, rare plants to thrive, such as orange bird's foot and dwarf pansy. Within Britain, both grow only on Scilly, so they are special.

Leave East Porth, heading south for 200m before curving left (east) to paddle around the south side of Crump Island. From here, it is a further 300m to the swathes of grainy white sand that line the shores of the island of St Martin's. Make for the concrete slipway that provides access to the ambitiously named Lower Town (one of three communities on St Martin's).

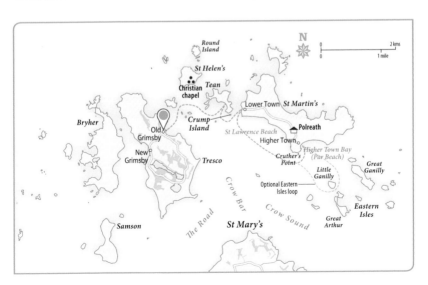

Rather than landing, continue southeast for 2.5km (1½ miles), roughly tracing the magnificent shoreline that takes in views of the wide, pristine beach of St Lawrence, backed by tall, swaying palm trees. Bend round the small headland at the southern tip of the island (Cruther's Point) and you'll be brought to yet another exotic-looking beach that marks your arrival in Higher Town Bay (aka Par Beach) – the gateway to the Eastern Isles.

Here, you can either kick back and enjoy a relaxing picnic on this calmest of shorelines or wander up the slipway and into Higher Town itself for a bite to eat.

↑ Paddling across Tresco Channel, crossing from Tresco to St Martin's. (Bob Carr)

The 120 denizens of St Martin's are a productive and creative bunch: Higher Town even includes a flower farm and a vineyard, both open to visitors.

There are a few options from this point. You could retrace your route to Tresco, catch one of the daily inter-island boats (but you must be mindful of tides and timings) or, if you're an experienced paddler (see *Titbits* below) you might indulge in a horseshoe-shaped paddle of 3km (2 miles) out to the rugged Eastern Isles and back. These rocky islets are remote and visited by few people; both locals and conservationists like to keep it that way. You are not permitted to land, so stay on the water.

Keep alert and you should spot Atlantic grey seals basking on the rocks or lolling in the shallows. The seal colony is resident, and spending time with these inquisitive creatures has provided some of my most treasured memories of the Scilly Isles. On one unforgettable occasion, I swam with seals that decided to nibble my fins and bite my goggles. Although it may seem intimidating getting quite so personal with a wild animal, there is no need for you to be alarmed. The seals are simply using their teeth and whiskers to judge textures and to work out what you are. Once you or the seals have had enough, head back to St Martin's, then take one of the options available to return to Tresco.

GETTING THERE

For details on getting to and around the Isles of Scilly, see page 25.

HIRE & LESSONS

Bennett Boatyard on Bryher (⌗ bennettboatyard.com) offers kayak and board hire and can drop off to other islands (including Tresco) if booked in advance.

WHERE TO STAY & EAT

On St Martin's, Polreath (⌗ polreath.com) in Higher Town combines a quaint tearoom and guesthouse. At Lower Town, Karma (⌗ tinyurl.com/karma-st-martins) is a luxury hotel offering holistic treatments. Other accommodation options are at ⌗ stmartinsscilly.co.uk/places-to-stay.html. Eateries in Higher Town include Adam's Fish and Chips (⌗ adamsfishandchips.co.uk) and The Island Bakery (⌗ theislandbakery-stmartins.com). On Tresco, Ruin Beach Café is close to the start/finish point (⌗ tresco.co.uk/eating-on-tresco/ruin-café).

TITBITS

Remember that the Isles of Scilly front the Atlantic, so conditions can be tough. On this route, the Eastern Isles are particularly exposed, and their waters should only be attempted by experienced paddlers or with a guide. Check conditions before completing.

3 A WORLD APART

PADDLE AROUND A COVE THAT STRADDLES A GEOLOGICAL FAULT LINE SPLITTING THE LIZARD FROM CORNWALL

WHERE	The Lizard, Cornwall
STATS	↔→ n/a (free paddle) ②
START/FINISH	Porthallow Cove ♀ SW797232

The truth is, paddling anywhere on the coast of Cornwall will send your senses into glorious chaos. And, unlike its sister county Devon, where the north and south coast are set too far apart, Cornwall's opposite coastlines are sufficiently proximate to hop between. So you can readily sample both in a single day.

In the morning, you might choose to test your paddling strength and balance on Cornwall's wild north coast before a quick afternoon trip over to the River Fal and its creeks and ancient woodlands (page 42), or to Roseland's hidden creeks fed by the River Fal. If that's not enough, why not throw in a paddle round any of the stunning coves and secluded beaches that stipple the county's south coast? After all, you don't need to constrain yourself to a single compass point when you can easily do more than one. Throw in wooded river valleys, cute fishing villages and historic castles, and you can well understand why 'grockles' flock here in their millions every year.

Even amid this embarrassment of riches, a few paddling spots stand out as particularly favourable. Take Porthallow, a sheltered cove on the east flank of the Lizard Peninsula, a landmass that extends to become the

↑ Another successful paddle off the Cornish coast. (SUP in a Bag/Classic Cottages)

most southerly point in Britain. The cove's position offers uninterrupted views east along the English Channel and makes it a secluded little haven.

But Porthallow is a lot more than just a pretty Cornish bay. It forms part of a geological Site of Special Scientific Interest, because it lies on the Lizard Boundary Faultline that marks the collision of tectonic plates 300 million years ago. Accordingly, it is a popular spot for rock-studying and -loving folk.

The pebbly cove of Porthallow is relatively sheltered from the prevailing southwesterly winds – certainly less blowy than the Atlantic-facing side of The Lizard. Offering a crystal-clear sea backed by a small village, this is an idyllic spot and thus the perfect base for watersport enthusiasts.

PADDLE THIS WAY

Start on the shores of Porthallow Cove and – simply – explore. This excursion is all about freedom, about following up whatever intrigues you or catches your eye. There is no right or wrong way to enjoy this sumptuous little bay. That said, here are some ideas and pointers that, depending on the wind direction and strength, may be worth weaving into your individual choice of route.

Particularly if the breeze hails from the south, head north as the tailwind will give you a little thrust along the jagged coastline. (Just remember, however, that any waterborne return will involve paddling into a headwind.) The first bay to the north, less than 500m (⅓ mile) on, is Nelly's Cove. The boulder-rich cliffs that back the bay offer two sets of benefits. Not only do they protect it from a lot of wind but they also foster a sense of seclusion. This is an ideal combination for a peaceful picnic lunch, accompanied by gentle murmurings from waves tickling your feet.

The shoreline of Nelly's Cove mixes shingle and scattered rocks, so be mindful

↑ Pick your way carefully across Porthallow's stony beach to reach the launch point. (Helen Hotson/S)

of catching your fin as you approach the shallows. While I barely ventured further than Nelly's Cove on my visit, instead enjoying views of land from the sea, you might wish to paddle further north along the coast to another couple of coves, namely Fletching's and Nare's. Beyond the latter lies Nare Point, a headland that curves west and leads into the Helford River where you can enjoy an altogether different paddle (page 38).

If the winds are northerly, or even northeasterly, you might prioritise heading south to Porthkerris. It's a short paddle (500m or ⅓ mile) but this journey isn't about 'beasting it' along the coast. Instead, take time to absorb the peace and calm as the waves loll around you and the skies shift above your head (which may be graced by a party of chough, ragamuffin crows that have recently returned to The Lizard). There is a small bay at Porthkerris Cove, a popular departure spot for scuba divers heading out to The Manacles, a rocky reef that forms one of the UK's best dive spots. Notice the little white cabin on the cove shores? This is Porthkerris Beach Café, which has been referred to as the 'southernmost place [in Britain] to get a decent cup of coffee'. It's perfect for a quick caffeine hit before you make your way back to your starting point.

GETTING THERE

From Helston, take the A3083 south then turn southeast on the B3293 to St Keverne, from where you follow minor roads northeast to Porthallow. Public parking is available on the beach and voluntary donations welcomed to fund upkeep of the area. Unfortunately, public transport is not practical here.

HIRE & LESSONS

Based in Truro, the brilliantly named SUP In A Bag (⌗ supinabag.co.uk) rents equipment including multi-day hires, with free delivery; they even do handovers on the A30 if that is on your route. The company also offers guided SUP tours of the coast and even holidays.

WHERE TO STAY & EAT

In Porthallow, The Five Pilchards Inn (⌗ thefivepilchards.co.uk) combines a bar, restaurant and B&B. On the edge of Porthallow, Gallen-Treath Guest House (⌗ gallen-treath.com) is cheap and cheerful. Porthkerris Beach Café is a must-visit (⌗ tinyurl.com/porthkerris-cafe). For something a little heartier head to St Keverne (a short but beautiful walk away) and visit The White Hart (⌗ thewhitehartstkeverne.co.uk).

TITBITS

Porthallow Cove is precisely midway along the South West Coast Path, which runs between Poole (Dorset) and Minehead (Somerset). Have a look for the stone halfway marker that is on the beach.

4 SEA SAFARI

A CORNISH COASTAL ROUTE THAT DEMANDS MASK & SNORKEL AS WELL AS PADDLE

WHERE	Penzance, Cornwall
STATS	↔ 8km (6¼ miles) round trip ③
START/FINISH	Mount's Bay 📍 SW506312

t's fair to say that a safari, in its traditional sense, isn't something we can expect from Britain. But think slightly differently in terms of wildlife-rich adventures, and you'll discover that this country has much to offer. Nowhere is this truer than the abundance of 'sea safari' opportunities that throng the southwest coast of England. So it's time to start swotting up on how to tell your shags from your cormorants, and differentiate your blennies from your gobies.

This excursion thus involves looking both up (at the sky) and peering down (into the sea). The dramatic skylines of the Cornish cliffs are home to ample breeding seabirds around whose colonies you might spot a mighty peregrine bombing. Arguably, though, the most excitement comes from donning a mask and sticking your head underwater, beneath your board. In the more sheltered spots, where the water is glassy, a keen eye may discern a spiny starfish (with three rows of spines on each of its five 'arms'). In summer or early autumn, you may even luck out and encounter a jellyfish 'bloom'. Compass jellyfish are a common species,

↑ The island of St Michael's Mount dominates the view at Mount's Bay. How can you not want to paddle there? (SS)

but barrel jellyfish (which can be the size of dustbin lids) have also been seen here. If you want to get even closer to the action bring your snorkel and slip under the swell – just don't get stung! It's worth keeping an eye out for seals bobbing in the wave like enormous corks. The UK is a global stronghold for Atlantic grey seals, holding 40% of the world's estimated population of 600,000. Even better, they are an almost common sight off the Cornish coast. Further offshore, there's a decent chance of dolphins – usually short-beaked common but occasionally Risso's – and from early summer until the autumn the enormous but docile basking sharks are known to show their dorsal and tail fins (if not their faces).

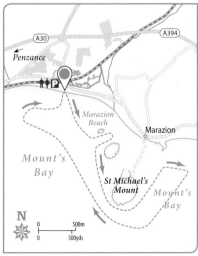

Mount's Bay, shaped like a half-moon, is vast and sweeping, spanning from The Lizard (page 30) west to Gwennap Head, which lies close to Land's End. Mount's Bay is heralded for cetaceans and is the best place in Britain to see harbour porpoise in decent numbers, with day-counts sometimes reaching three figures. You might also hope to see minke and humpback whales, which both make sporadic appearances along the Cornish coastline. In 2016, there was even a remarkable record of a bowhead whale (a very rare Arctic species).

In the north of the bay near Marazion, the island of St Michael's Mount is an obvious landmark. During winter gales, in particular, it can be dangerous – so if you paddle that way, take care. The waters are peppered with more than 150 shipwrecks. On the plus side, the 2016 designation of a Marine Conservation Zone around the area bodes well for wildlife conservation.

PADDLE THIS WAY

Launch anywhere along the long, wide blanket of grainy sand that makes up the rather peaceful shoreline of Mount's Bay. Then head due east towards St Michael's Mount, the small island sitting a sanguine distance from the shores. As you approach, watch the Mount's castle grow larger and more imposing. Notice too the Cornish flag flying from its periphery – a white cross on a black background. The standard derives from that of St Piran, who – so legend tells – was smelting tin when the molten white metal formed the shape of a cross on his black hearthstone.

From St Michael's Mount, paddle from west to east curving the southern fringe of the island, past the popular tourist spot of Marazion, looking out for the varied sealife that lives below, around and above the surface. Once you clear the east side of the island, continue to explore eastwards for more marine-life spotting before making your way back to base via roughly the same route.

GETTING THERE

Penzance sits at the southwestern tip of the A30, around 80km (50 miles) beyond Bodmin. Leave the A30 east of town, at the roundabout for Marazion. Head south and use the beach car park (♥ SW506312). Penzance is served by trains from London and South Wales (including a nightly sleeper service from London Paddington).

HIRE & LESSONS

Based in Marazion, The Hoxton Special (⟨⟩ thehoxtonspecial.com) offers lessons.

WHERE TO STAY & EAT

As befits a major town in a tourist Mecca of a county, Penzance offers many options for eating. Situated at the harbour, The Boat Shed (⟨⟩ boatshedpz.co.uk) is renowned for its locally caught seafood. Accommodation options are collated at ⟨⟩ penzance.co.uk/accommodation/index.htm.

↑ Keep an eye out for the fins of basking sharks breaking the surface of Cornish waters in summer. (SS)

5 HEAVENLY HELFORD

PADDLE IN PEACE ALONG A TRANQUIL CORNISH RIVER

WHERE	Helford River, Cornwall
STATS	←→ 10km (6¼ miles) return ②
START/FINISH	Ford in Helford village ♀ SW758262

The village of Helford crams a lot of personality and some serious history into its small size. Nestled quietly between Falmouth Bay to the north and the Lizard Peninsula to the south (page 30), the River Helford is equally as impressive as its neighbours.

Helford's shoreline is varied and enchanting. Intrepid paddlers have plenty to explore: quaint villages and secluded beaches, quiet coves and peaceful creeks. Helford village could hardly be more quintessentially English, with its thatched cottages, boathouses and historic features (including an old red phone box). Now a peaceful retreat, the Helford was once a thriving industrial and agricultural trade route for mines, quarries and farms as well as local fishermen. There at least, little has changed: fishermen still land their daily catch on the river's shoreline.

↑ The peaceful Cornish village of Helford marks your starting point. (chrisatpps/S)

Helford is well known for its hidden creeks. The most renowned is Frenchman's Creek, which secured fame in Daphne Du Maurier's novel of the same name. Sitting upstream of the suggested paddle route, this quiet wooded creek brims with wild garlic and bluebells in spring.

Gillan Creek, the destination favoured in this chapter, is equally beautiful. Fringed with trees, its steep sides rise sharply. On its narrow muddy margins, look out for little egrets (which only properly arrived in Britain less than 30 years ago, but are now common and widespread) and grey herons, which fish stealthily and surprisingly unobtrusively.

As for coves, try Bosahan. This small rocky bay lolls between Helford and Gillan Creek and is certainly worth a second (and third) glance. Even better, dedicate some quality time to unveil its unusual charm. Instead of lofty cliffs offering shelter, the shrub-layered rocks of this quiet hollow impart the sense of an enchanted woodland. As is the (brilliant!) norm among Cornish coves, Bosahan is quite the picture-perfect picnic spot. Just one word of caution: be aware that recent landslides have left the ground quite unstable and rocky in some locations.

Striking though the rock formations in the outer Helford may be, but innocent they are not. Unseen and thus dangerous protrusions in the river, estuary and bay have wrecked many a vessel. In 1891, the *Bay of Panama*, a steel barque heading from Calcutta to Dundee, was caught in a storm and blown on to Helford rocks. In 1920, *Rock Island Bridge,* an American cargo ship, was damaged in dense fog and wrecked. Some good has come of these and other ships' tragic demise, however, as they have become very popular with divers, some of whom never relinquish hope of finding treasure!

PADDLE THIS WAY

This route is best timed for a couple of hours before high tide, as both Helford and Gillan creeks dry out at low tide – and you don't want to get stuck in mud. Launch from the ford south of the small wooden bridge in Helford village, then head downstream (east) towards Falmouth Bay. As you approach Helford River Sailing Club you'll weave through anchored boats bobbing in the water. It can sometimes be tricky to navigate between these – particularly if it is windy

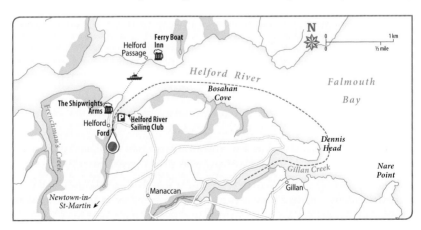

or extremely busy – but they certainly add charm and texture to this already picturesque paddle. Summer is sailing season, so during those warmer months many a sailor may doff his or her cap to you or give you a friendly wave.

As the river widens into Falmouth Bay the comforting effect of the sheltering shoreline quickly drops away and the elements enter more keenly into play. To mitigate the impact of the wind, stay close to the river's southern shore rather than paddle into mid-channel (let alone attempt to cross to the north bank of the river, as you would be making particularly hard work for yourself). Roughly 1.5km (1 mile) east of Helford, you'll see the secluded Bosahan Cove among the steep rocky banks on your right. It is easily discerned by its shrubby green backdrop – rather than the usual crags you've been seeing. Jump off and explore – or simply relax and nibble on a picnic. Return to the water, heading further east down the coast, past jagged stacks and outcrops.

Past Bosahan Cove you will reach a rocky headland pushing out east from the mainland. This is Dennis Head; it marks the entrance to Gillan Creek, one of few side channels off the Helford River. Arc right here so that you are paddling pretty much west before jinking southwest. Paddling upstream, notice that the steep creek sides are topped with trees, and allow the quietness of your surroundings to reveal the songs and calls of birds. Take a moment to revel in the views and sounds, and to regain your breath. At low tide Gillan Creek dries out so keep this in mind as you decide how far up the way you want to travel. When you're ready, head back to Helford, following the route in reverse, perhaps stopping on your way back to explore the small cove, backed by mature woodland, 300m southeast of Bosahan.

↑ Kayaking along the mirror-like Helford River. (Koru Kayaking)

GETTING THERE

Southeast of Helston, leave the A3083 east on to the B3293, then follow minor roads via Newtown-in-St Martin to reach Helford. Use the public car park by Helford River Sailing Club (⊘ helfordriversailingclub. co.uk). If you join the Club's holiday membership scheme (£50/family for two weeks), you may launch from here and use Club facilities including restaurant and showers. Otherwise, launch from the ford by a small wooden bridge that is 2 minutes' walk from the car park. Unfortunately, public transport is not realistic here – although you could conceivably get a train to Falmouth, then a taxi from there.

HIRE & LESSONS

SUP In A Bag (⊘ supinabag.co.uk; see also page 33) rents equipment and offers guided tours. For kayakers, Koru Kayaking (⊘ korukayaking.co.uk) offers guided kayak tours, specialising in the Helford River.

WHERE TO STAY & EAT

A charming thatched pub in Helford, The Shipwrights Arms (⊘ shipwrightshelford. co.uk) overlooks the river; in summer, you'll likely see families crabbing off the slipway. On the north side of the river (reached by a passenger ferry in summer, which saves a fair drive round), the Ferry Boat Inn (⊘ ferryboatcornwall.co.uk) in Helford Passage is a 300-year-old pub offering accommodation and food amid magnificent surroundings of wooded banks and sloping fields.

→ Grey herons are a regular sight along the shores of the Helford River. (James Lowen)

6 THREE IN ONE

INVESTIGATE A TRIO OF TRANQUIL RIVERS THAT PAY HOMAGE TO CORNWALL'S MARITIME & METALLIC HISTORY

WHERE	Rivers Truro, Fal and Tresillian, Cornwall
STATS	↔ 7.5km (4½ miles) one-way ② – ③
START	Roundwood Quay, Coombe ♥ SW840404
FINISH	Tresillian ♥ SW865461

The River Fal separates the Roseland Peninsula from the rest of Cornwall and connects upstream with the River Truro and, later, the Tresillian River. About halfway along the riverine route connecting Truro and Falmouth is Roundwood Quay, which lies where Lamouth and Cowland creeks drift east into the River Fal, just south of the Fal's union with the River Truro. During the 18th century – the heyday of Cornwall's trade in tin and copper – ships docked at Roundwood Quay. Even today, the quay's granite walls, quoins and capping stones remain intact. For those who prefer their history older, the remains of an Iron Age fort grace the woods back from the quay.

Start to paddle along the wide, glistening waters of the Fal, however, and you'll soon forget the area's metallic past. Keep your eye out for interesting and wonderful wildlife. You may glimpse shoaling fish or the neon bolt of a kingfisher hurtling past. On the muddy, invertebrate-rich shores unveiled by a falling tide, you may sight curlews or (the less well-known) black-tailed godwits, whose population on the Fal is of national (bordering international) significance. There are plenty of opportunities to pause and picnic too, thanks to the presence of several, enticing shingle beaches. Best of all, you can rejoice in the tranquillity of this part of the estuary – full of hidden nooks and secluded crannies – and all seemingly a world away from the buzz of Cornwall's tourist hotspots.

PADDLE THIS WAY

Launch from the slipway on Roundwood Quay, ideally setting out on a low tide to take advantage of the flood (incoming) tide making for a gentler paddle. If you are

↑ A burning evening sky above Truro cathedral, as viewed from Malpas. (Ian Woolcock/S)

planning a round paddle then aim to journey back on the ebb. Turn immediately south, heading east until you reach the main channel. After 1km (⅔ mile), the Fal continues straight but you bear left (north) along the Truro River. After 3km (2 miles) – admiring the fulsome woodland that comes right down to the mud – you reach the charming village of Malpas. Here, a beautiful pub, The Heron Inn, sits boldly on the banks at a watery fork that marks the junction between the Truro River (which heads left, or northwest) and the Tresillian River (which bears right, northeast). Were you to continue up the Truro River you would reach the eponymous town. Bear right (northeast) and wind along the Tresillian River. At low tide, the river here is confined to a narrow channel that weaves through mudflats fringed by woods and fields. The main public footpath deviates from the river at Malpas, cutting inland until it rejoins the Tresillian 1.7km (1 mile) on at

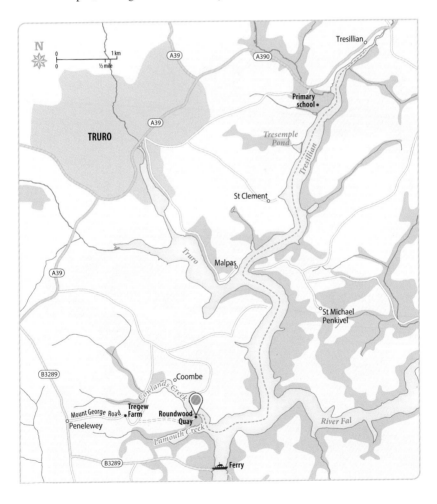

↑ Passing St Clement village announces that you are in the final third of the paddle. (Helen Hotson/S)

St Clement. This leaves the shore marvellously free of walkers for a consequently most tranquil stretch. But don't be fooled into thinking you're completely alone. From egrets and gulls to swans and waders, birdlife is particularly noticeable along the Tresillian.

Continue northeast, sticking to the main channel – particularly on a falling tide – to avoid being stuck on mudbanks. A little over 2km (1¼ miles) beyond St Clement, Tresemple Pond appears on your left. At low tide, mallards abound. If you visit in the breeding season, you may see females with flotillas of chicks. Should it be playtime at the adjacent primary school that is hidden among the mixed old oak, coppiced hazel and pines, the ducks' quacking may be accompanied by the subdued hum of laughter mixed with occasional excited cries.

On the approach to Tresillian village, you will reach a small slipway on the left (west) bank, coupled with a line of reedbeds. The murmuring of those slender plants signals a sad truth: the start of the end. Retrace your route downriver to Roundwood Quay.

GETTING THERE

Take the A39 south from Truro towards Falmouth. At Playing Place, turn southeast on to the B3289 (signposted to the National Trust property at Trelissick Garden). After 1.5km (1 mile), at Penelewey, turn east on to Mount George Road, which leads to Tregew Farm. From here, the road deteriorates into a track that bumps 1km (⅔ mile) to the parking area at Roundwood Quay. (This last section is too rough for cars with a low suspension. You may prefer to park near Tregew Farm and walk the rest.)

HIRE & LESSONS

Located in Falmouth, WeSUP Paddleboard Centre (⌂ wesup.co.uk) rents equipment, arranges guided tours and offers lessons.

WHERE TO STAY & EAT

In Penelewey, just north of where you turn off the B3289 to reach Roundwood Quay, The Punchbowl and Ladle (⌂ punchbowlandladle.com) is a 15th-century thatched pub serving good food. On the river's edge at Malpas, The Heron Inn (⌂ heroninnmalpas.co.uk) serves locally sourced food. In St Clement, The Old Vicarage (⌂ theoldvicaragetruro.co.uk) is a smart guesthouse in a 15th-century house on the shores of the Tresillian River.

TITBITS

The waters around Roundwood Quay and south towards Carrick Roads (and beyond) are popular with pleasure boats, especially in summer. Stay vigilant and ensure you are competent at manoeuvring the board efficiently and at speed, if needed.

7 SOUTHWESTERN SUNDOWNER

BUMBLE AROUND THE SMALL CAVES, ROCKY OUTCROPS & REMOTE BEACHES OF PORTMELLON

WHERE	Portmellon, Cornwall
STATS	←→ n/a: just have a paddle! ②
START/FINISH	Portmellon Cove ♀ SX016438

D ue east of Truro, and sufficiently close to the River Fal (page 42) to justify combining into a hedonistic weekend of paddling, is Portmellon Cove. Sited roughly 1.5km (1 mile) south of Mevagissey village, this is a gem of a place for paddling – deliciously off the beaten track, relaxingly quiet, and with ample opportunities for adventure, should the whim so take you. Not much happens here, and the locals like it that way.

Although still on Cornwall's south coast, the bay faces east into the English Channel, so is largely sheltered from the prevailing Atlantic-generated winds. Portmellon is simply the perfect place for remote relaxation interspersed with exploring nearby hidden beaches and small caves.

PADDLE THIS WAY

The cove itself has a sandy beach with gorgeous, sparklingly clear and shallow water. The ethos of this chapter – playing things by ear – means that I'm not going to propose a specific route for you to follow – so don't go looking for a line marking the route on the map to the right.

Instead, if conditions are benign, launch from the slipway on Portmellon Beach and simply follow the coastline around to the north towards Mevagissey and beyond. Go prepared with a picnic, then enjoy a couple of hours' isolation, coming ashore to escape on whatever picturesque, evocatively named beach takes your fancy – perhaps Little Polsreath or Cockaluney?

You might not quite be on your own, however. You may spot a seal bobbing in the swell, only its head visible and what surely passes for a satisfied smirk on whiskered chops.

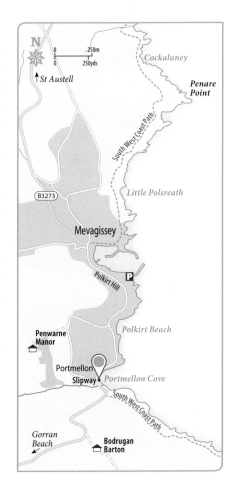

← The coast either side of Mevagissey has several beaches that demand your exploration. (JMAV/S)

With its harbour and stacks of houses, Mevagissey is the perfect Cornish village. (Mike

GETTING THERE

Take the A390 to St Austell, then head south on the B3273 to Mevagissey. From here take a minor road (called Polkirt Hill) south to reach Portmellon. Use the car park behind the Rising Sun Inn (♀ SX015440), which fronts the cove. Walk to the slipway to launch. Nearest train station is St Austell, from where you can take bus 24 to Trevarth, then walk 1.6km (1 mile) to Portmellon.

HIRE & LESSONS

Haven Kayaks (⟳ havenkayaks.net) is based just south at Goran Haven Beach, and rent kayaks and paddleboards.

WHERE TO STAY & EAT

In Portmellon, The Rising Sun Inn (⟳ therisingsuninn.com) is a 17th-century pub offering superb views across the cove from a privileged water's-edge position. It serves traditional pub food and local ales. There is accommodation too; if the night ends clear, you'll discover the reason for the east-facing pub's name. Other accommodation options nearby include self-catering at both Penwarne Manor (⟳ penwarnemanor.co.uk) and Bodrugan Barton (⟳ bodrugan.co.uk). Both are converted 16th-century manors that used to house noble families. There are also rumours that Penwarne holds a secret tunnel that leads all the way to the coast!

TITBITS

If the wind is from the east, Portmellon is nicely sheltered. It only takes an easterly or a spring tide to shake things up, however — so do keep an eye on the weather.

8 AND THEN THERE WERE NONE

PADDLE BETWEEN SANDY BEACHES GUARDED BY ROCKY OUTCROPS & EXPLORE AGATHA CHRISTIE'S FAVOURITE ISLAND

WHERE	Bigbury Bay, Devon
STATS	←→ 12km (7½ miles) return ③
START/FINISH	Bigbury-on-Sea ♀ SX651441

The South Devon coast hosts a substantial segment of England's longest National Trail, the 1,000km (630 mile) South West Coast Path that runs from Minehead in Somerset to Poole Harbour in Dorset. The path snakes through a World Heritage Site and a national park as well as visiting fishing villages, topping rugged cliffs and admiring perfectly secluded little bays. Immersing yourself on the trail by foot is one thing, but observing the stunning coastline from the water is an altogether different experience. The section between Bigbury Bay and South Milton Sands luxuriating in the South Devon Area of Outstanding Natural Beauty, and formerly a thriving pilchard-fishing area – is particularly lovely. Here glorious sandy beaches occupy sheltered coves that are fringed by sharp rocks, and rolling green fields press inland.

This stretch of coast focuses on the tidal island of Burgh. Once the refuge of pirates and smugglers, it is today dominated by a famous Art Deco-style hotel that inspired two Agatha Christie novels (it serves as Soldier Island in *And Then There Were None* and crops up again in the Hercule Poirot mystery *Evil Under the Sun*). The island also has the remains of a chapel known as the 'Huer's Hut', believed to be an old watchpoint for fishermen looking for shoals of pilchard. Once seen, the 'huer' would make a 'hue and cry' to alert others around Bigbury.

↑ Bigbury Bay's rocky pinnacles: best admired from a safe distance. (SS)

PADDLE THIS WAY

Launch from the golden sands of Bigbury Bay, ideally at high tide in order to circumnavigate Burgh Island. Sitting 400m (¼ mile) from the mainland, the

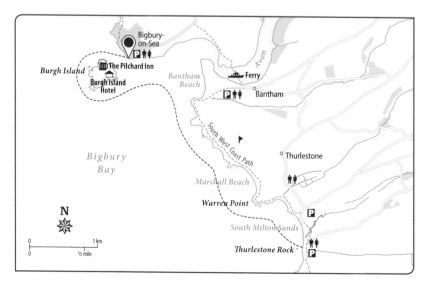

island is tiny (just 250m²). You can walk across at low tide. At high tide, a third-generation hydraulic sea-tractor – reputedly the only one in the world – transports visitors across but it's more fun to race the vehicle on your paddleboard.

Unlike motorised boats, paddleboards can access Burgh Island via a slipway on the east of the island. Spend a while exploring the island's varied terrain. Its small size belies considerable character – which is doubtless why Agatha Christie was doubly inspired. Rugged rocks dominate but release your inner Daryl Hannah by checking out the 'Mermaid Pool' – a seawater pool surrounded by hefty boulders – on the southeastern shore. Then return to your board to circumnavigate the island, which enables you to explore small caves and inlets scattered around its perimeter. Such an intimate examination – with the vastness of the Atlantic Ocean at your back – exemplifies the unique and very tangible pleasure that can only come from discovering a place in such a unique (waterborne and self-propelled) way.

Leave Burgh Island eastwards, keeping the large expanse of Bantham Beach to your left (east) and continue tracking the coastline southeast for 2km (1¼ miles)

↑ Arriving at Burgh Island by kayak. (SS)

to reach Marshall Beach. This shingle cove is accessible only by water or via the coastal footpath, which makes it a secluded spot to paddle ashore – should the inclination so take you – and admire the ocean views in solitude.

If you paused at Marshall Beach, be mindful of the rocks as you leave as there may be some shallow shards ready to catch a fin. Follow the staggered line of dark, bulging rocks and cliffs that loom to your left (north) as you trace the shoreline southeast for 1.5km (1 mile) until the coast rounds Warren Point and curves inland. Here it cedes to a long sweep of creamy sand edged by low green hills – the sheltered bay of South Milton Sands. Keep an eye out for seals, which are regularly spotted flirting with the waves here.

Head ashore just below the Beachhouse (a café), immediately east of the iconic arch of Thurlestone Rock. At low tide, this is a popular place to go rockpooling near the iconic arch. Look out for limpets, anemones, shore crabs, pipe fish, sea scorpions, spiny stars, Cornish suckers (also known as clingfish) and edible crabs, which all reside here and are trapped in rocky 'tanks' by the retreating tide. Just make sure you leave enough time, and tide, to make the return journey north to Bigbury Bay.

Head back towards Burgh Island, perhaps stopping by en route to Bigbury to reward your efforts with a drink at The Pilchard Inn. This 14th-century hideout for smugglers and pirates lies at the foot of the island. Here, on a summer's day, you can sit on wooden tables outside overlooking Bigbury Bay and savour a well-earned glass of something cold.

GETTING THERE

Turn off the A379 just southeast of Modbury, heading south along the B3392, following signs to Burgh Island and Bigbury-on-Sea. Use the car park by the beach (♀ SX651442) then walk south to the coast. Nearest train station is Plymouth, from where you can catch bus 885 to Bigbury-on-Sea or take a taxi.

HIRE & LESSONS

Discovery Surf School (⌀ discoverysurf.com) is located in Bigbury-on-Sea. It offers surf and SUP lessons and rents boards.

WHERE TO STAY & EAT

Burgh Island Hotel (⌀ burghisland.com) offers fancy accommodation and dining. Its owners also run The Pilchard Inn, which has been quenching the island's thirst for seven centuries. Definitely worth a visit, if for no other reason than to say you've been. On South Milton Sands, Beachhouse (⌀ beachhousedevon.com) is a café with a relaxed vibe, specialising in seafood and offering a takeaway menu.

9 BULLSEYE

PADDLE A RIVERINE MICROCOSM OF BRITAIN — WOODLAND, ROLLING HILLS & HISTORIC BUILDINGS

WHERE	River Dart, Devon
STATS	←→ 15km (9 ⅓ miles) one-way ① – ②
START	Dart–Totnes Rowing Club, Totnes ♀ SX809596
FINISH	Dartmouth Boat Hire, Dartmouth ♀ SX879514

If you were asked to describe the quintessential English river, what you would come up with probably would look pretty much like the River Dart. Grand homes are secreted among rolling hills. Open pastures cosset boathouses while sailing boats young and old are sprinkled across the water. An impressive diversity of wildlife calls this perfect waterway home. And we haven't broached the Dart's thousand years of history – or supped a pint of local ale. Paddling doesn't get much better.

The name 'Dart' seems to be derived from a Celtic word meaning 'where oak trees grow'. And flourish here they do, mature trees voluptuously cosseting the river along its lower course. The River Dart rises on the uplands of Dartmoor and becomes tidal by the time it reaches Totnes, a quirky town with a 17th-century weir. Set in the Dart Valley, revelling in alternative cultures and watched over by one of Britain's best-preserved motte-and-bailey castles, Totnes must be among one of the coolest places in England to start a paddle.

PADDLE THIS WAY

Launch from the public slipway next to the Dart–Totnes Rowing Club on Steamer Quay. Start on the high tide, taking the ebb down. The river starts straight and narrow, before you begin winding through tall oak forest. The proximity to the

↑ The village of Kingswear, viewed from south of Dartmouth, at the end of the paddle. (SS)

banks means that any wildlife you see will be very close. If you like birds, you'll have a ball: look for kingfishers, buzzards and little egrets; you may even chance upon a transient osprey refuelling here on its journey north or south.

After 2.5km (1½ miles), look out for Sharpham House, a Grade-1-listed Georgian manor that hosts mindfulness retreats and harbours an award-winning vineyard, which overlooks a bend in the river on your right (west). At Stoke Point, another 2.5km (1½ miles) downstream and slightly north of Bow Creek (which arrives from the west), the river starts to open out – and everything changes.

Gone is the seclusion of the opening section. Now the vista expands, with views across vast open hills, and boat traffic starts to increase. In places the river is up to 1km (⅔ mile) wide. While the glistening waters look spectacular when the sun reflects off them, they can get rather choppy – so stay focused.

About 500m (⅓ mile) beyond Stoke Point is a small entrance to a hidden creek. Paddle through to reach a peaceful mill pond that houses Stoke Gabriel,

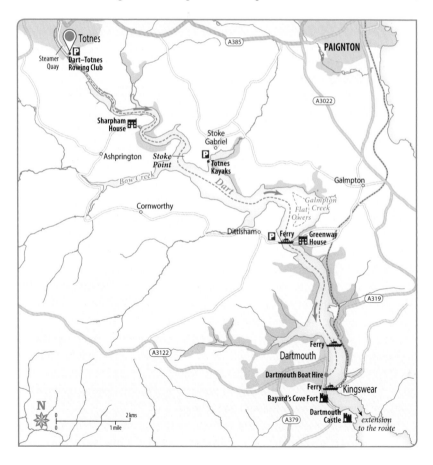

a village fringed by trees through which a church spire peeks out. Look left (east), up Galmpton Creek where boathouses smatter the riverbank, and you'll see Galmpton village, a holding area for landing craft before the D-Day landings in World War II. If you have ever been tempted to live on a river, gliding past these boathouses (and perhaps peering in, albeit respectfully) will decide you! Here, on the east of the river, lays an area of exposed sand at low tide known as Flat Owers that is best avoided by sticking to the middle of the channel – easily done given this section of the river has widened considerably compared with the start.

Just beyond Galmpton and on the opposite (west) bank lies Dittisham, an unspoilt riverside settlement that traces its history back to a Saxon invasion in AD660. Back on the east bank, peer over at Greenway House, once Agatha Christie's holiday home. Atlantic grey seals are regularly spotted in these parts. If you're brave enough to take a dip (this is a popular 'wild swimming' haunt too), they are quite inquisitive. Nevertheless, please be patient and respectful. Allow seals to approach you rather than pursuing them. After Dittisham the river narrows again and woodland returns to its banks.

Once at Dartmouth you have three options. First, wait for the flood tide to accelerate your return north. Second, take a well-deserved rest and hop aboard the Dartmouth–Totnes river cruise back to Totnes. Or perhaps you want to carry on? I don't blame you; it's stunning in these parts. Option three is therefore to continue beyond the route marked on the map!

On the opposite (east) bank to Dartmouth sits Kingswear. There's no mistaking this town, for it comprises tiers of brightly painted houses that put even

↑ The River Dart at Totnes, where you start this paddle. (Philip Bird LRPS CPAGB/S)

Tobermory (or its fictional equivalent, Balamory) to shame. Turn your head the other way, looking west, and Bayard's Cove Fort attracts the eye. This Tudor defence contained heavy artillery to protect the then-prosperous harbour town from attack. A further sign of a tumultuous history lies 1km (⅔ mile) southeast. Dartmouth Castle is a 600-year-old fortress that once guarded the entrance to the Dart Estuary. From the water, it is quite some sight, with stone walls tumbling straight into the river below.

If you are an experienced paddler (and only if!), you may fancy venturing even further downstream – engaging with the rocky coast that announces the sea. You may even spot harbour porpoise. It is easy to lose track of time as you explore hidden coves and searing canyons – so keep an eye on both clock and weather. You don't want to be left stranded!

GETTING THERE

From the A38, take the A384 or A385 into Totnes. The most convenient car park is at the southeastern end of Steamer Quay (♥ SX809596). Launch from the adjacent Dart–Totnes Rowing Club (⚲ darttotnes. co.uk). Nearest train station is Totnes, from where it is roughly a 1km (⅔ mile) walk to the launch point. For public transport back from Dartmouth to Totnes, a convenient, paddleboard-friendly option is the ferry (⚲ dartmouthrailriver.co.uk/tours; ⏱ end Mar to end Oct).

HIRE & LESSONS

Paddleboards, canoes and kayaks can be hired from Totnes Kayaks (⚲ totneskayaks.co.uk) or Dittisham Boats (⚲ dittishamboats.co.uk). There are also options for lessons and guided excursions.

WHERE TO STAY & EAT

In Totnes, The Waterside Bistro (⚲ watersidebistro.com) offers simple but delicious breakfast, lunch and dinner menus. In Dittisham, The Anchorstone Café has a glorious riverside position (⚲ anchorstonecafe. co.uk) as does the old-style The Ferry Boat Inn (⚲ ferryboatinndittisham.pub). If you're a foodie then the award-winning Riverford Field Kitchen (⚲ fieldkitchen.riverford.co.uk) is a must. It's not on the paddling route – rather, 8km (5 miles) northwest of Totnes – so not easily accessible but if you're willing to go a little out of the way you won't be disappointed.

TITBITS

Be mindful of the ferries as you reach Dartmouth. The chain ferry cannot stop and you will need your wits about you to avoid causing any disruption. Also, if you are paddling on a spring tide, the water flows fast. When coupled with strong winds, this can generate breaking waves up to 1m in height. The Head of the Dart race (⚲ headofthedart.wordpress.com) takes place annually and sees paddlers journey from Totnes to Dartmouth (alternating direction each year). Book early as spaces are limited.

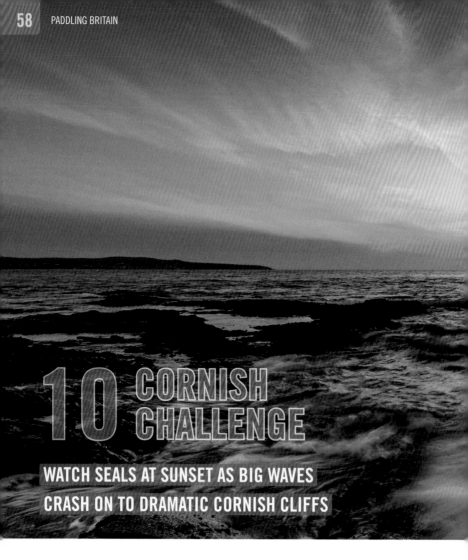

10 CORNISH CHALLENGE

WATCH SEALS AT SUNSET AS BIG WAVES CRASH ON TO DRAMATIC CORNISH CLIFFS

WHERE	Godrevy–Portreath Heritage Coast, Cornwall
STATS	←→ 11km (6¾ miles) one-way ⑤
START	St Ives Bay (south of Godrevy Point) ♀ SW581421
FINISH	Portreath Beach ♀ SW653454

The Godrevy–Portreath Heritage Coast provides everything you would want from Cornwall. There are dramatic cliffs and roaring Atlantic waves, hidden coves and tales of shipwrecks. At the northern tip of St Ives Bay, with 5km (3 miles) of golden sand linking it to the town of Hayle is Godrevy Point. Looking out to sea from here, you can see a 26m-tall, octagonal white lighthouse.

This stands proudly on Godrevy Island and warns of a submerged reef called The Stones that lies just offshore. The structure apparently inspired Virginia Woolf in *To the Lighthouse*, although the novel was

↑ The lighthouse on Godrevy Island inspired Virginia Woolf to write her novel *To the Lighthouse*. (Alina Cebula/S)

actually set on the Isle of Skye (page 226) in the Inner Hebrides of Scotland. The Stones claimed many human lives in the mid 19th century when passenger and cargo ships docked at St Ives.

Nowadays, Godrevy is instead frequented by gulls, oystercatchers, pipits and a resident colony of Atlantic grey seals. The last is one of the best reasons for coming here. Look for the seals resting on the shores of Mutton Cove at low tide, crooning loudly among themselves – indeed, you'll likely hear them first!

The UK hosts 40% of the world's Atlantic grey seals, and they are the country's heaviest mammal that spends at least part of the year on land. They are inquisitive creatures so don't be alarmed if they edge closer to you as you paddle, often ducking into the water and popping their head at ever-closer range as they grow more confident. Seals can be seen in any season, but occur in greater numbers during autumn and winter. From land, high cliffs make it hard to spot seals – making observing them from the water even more of a must. Also spotted, albeit more rarely, are harbour porpoise and (in summer) basking shark.

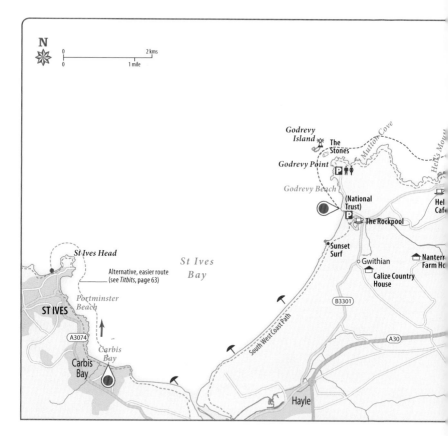

Behind the launch point on St Ives Bay are some prehistoric sites including an ancient burial ground. Look out for the rock stacks at Hell's Mouth, breeding grounds for seabirds such as guillemots, razorbills, kittiwakes and fulmars. Sometimes these whizz or swoop low, making for spectacular encounters. With its 100m-high cliffs, gorse-covered heath and rocky shoreline, this stretch of coast is, unsurprisingly, a designated Area of Outstanding Natural Beauty. But don't let the charming scenery lull you into a false sense of security: weather conditions can get quite wild here at times, and you should remain wary of The Stones reef.

PADDLE THIS WAY

Paddle hard – this one's a challenge! As with any coastal paddle, this route is no cinch, but it's well worth the effort. Launch from the north end of St Ives Bay, close to Godrevy Point. Keep the coast on your right (which is the east, initially, then north) throughout your paddle until you reach civilisation after 11km (8 miles), at Portreath village.

Rounding Godrevy Point you'll paddle past Godrevy Island lighthouse (to your northwest) then soon arrive at Mutton Cove, where with luck, you will see seals

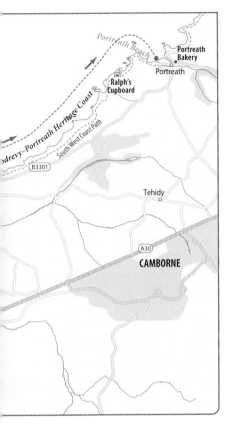

basking on the beach. On land, seals are far less confident so it's important to keep a safe distance from them. A clear sign that you have agitated seals is if they look up and around; should this happen, retreat.

Bar this first section of 1km (⅔ mile) or so, there aren't many particular landmarks along this jaunt, just 10km (6 miles) of superb rock formations and coves, some evocatively named. After 4km (2½ miles) of paddling you'll reach Hell's Mouth – a sequence of 100m-tall cliffs. Formerly a popular landing point for smugglers, today's users are seals. After a further 1km (⅔ mile), you reach Deadman's Cove. If nothing else, the name reinforces how perilous this stretch of coastline can be and stresses the level of competence needed for this paddle.

Head a further 3.5km (2¼ miles) beyond Deadman's Cove to reach the very impressive remains of a collapsed sea cave called Ralph's Cupboard. Legend has it that the occupant, Ralph, was an unpleasant character who took pleasure from wrecking passing ships so he could loot their cargo – which he then stowed in his rocky 'cupboard'. Venture through the gin-clear waters to explore – if you dare. Its narrow entry and steep sides create the sense of a somewhat claustrophobic amphitheatre. The cave echoes with the calls of birds circling above. The overall atmosphere veers on eerie. But it is worth it. Stumbling on little spots like this is a brilliant moment – what paddling is all about.

Pull into the beach at Portreath. If you've timed your arrival for late in the day, sit back and enjoy a glorious sunset. This is such a magnificent route that you might want to spend the night in Portreath and – weather permitting – paddle a return the following day.

→ Kittiwake, a smart-looking gull, breeds on the rocky cliffs at Hell's Mouth. (SS)

GETTING THERE

The launch point in St Ives Bay is northwest of the B3301, 7.4km (4½ miles) northeast of Hayle and 1.5km (1 mile) northwest of Gwithian. Use the National Trust car park (⦿ SW583422; ⦿ nationaltrust.org.uk/godrevy). There is a public car park (and public toilets) 1km (⅔ mile) further along the same track. The nearest train station is Hayle, which is so close to the water that you could drop your board into the water in St Ives Bay then paddle 1.5km (1 mile) along the beachfront to the suggested launch point.

HIRE & LESSONS

St Ives Surf School (⦿ stivessurfschool.co.uk) rents boards and provides lessons and guided tours for novice paddlers who seek a bit of a challenge. Gwithian Surf School (⦿ surfacademy.co.uk) also rents paddleboards. However, it could be argued that if you are renting equipment for this particular paddle, you may not be experienced enough to safely take it on!

WHEN TO GO

Summer offers longer daylight hours and more favourable conditions, but this route is all about timing the day right. To avoid hiccups, choose a day with glassy water and next-to-no breeze.

WHERE TO STAY & EAT

In Gwithian, Red River Inn (⦿ www.red-river-inn.com/location) offers an eclectic menu ranging from traditional pub food to Moroccan tagine and seared scallops. In Portreath, Atlantic Café Bar (⦿ theatlantictr16.co.uk) offers breakfasts, fish and chips, and other hot meals. Portreath Bakery (⦿ portreathbakery.co.uk) provides lighter options; perfect for

The rugged coast between Godrevy and Portreath is best appreciated from the sea. (SS)

picking something up to enjoy on the beach. The Rockpool (⊘ therockpoolbar.co.uk) is a small, laidback café in the dunes between Godrevy and Gwithian, where 'you're welcome to sit outside if your wetsuit hasn't dried out!'. Hell's Mouth Café (✆ 01209 718419) is a small coffee shop situated above the cove of the same name. In Hayle, Philps (⊘ philpspasties. co.uk) is justly famous for its amazing Cornish pasties.

B&Bs near Gwithian include Calize Country House (⊘ calize.co.uk) and Nanterrow Farm House (⊘ nanterrowfarm.co.uk). For camping, try Gwithian Farm (⊘ gwithianfarm.co.uk and Godrevy Park Caravan Club site (⊘ tinyurl.com/godrevy-park). West of Gwithian, Sunset Surf (⊘ sunset-surf.com) has a café and a B&B on the coast west of Gwithian.

TITBITS

This route is best avoided on a spring tide. Moreover, a deep channel by the lighthouse means that the current can be very fast. An outgoing tide pulls west and is best avoided. An incoming tide pulls east, towards Portreath, so try to take advantage of that. Be aware that once you pass Godrevy Point, high cliffs mean two things. First, there isn't really a safe exit until you reach Portreath. Second, you are no longer visible from the beach. Even if you do pull into a little cove for a short rest, you'll have to get back on water to reach civilisation again.

For less-experienced paddlers who wish to enjoy this glorious part of the British coastline, there is an easier option (also marked on the map). Set off from Carbis Bay, which is generally known for its flatter water and sheltered position. Head west towards St Ives Harbour, which is situated at the north end of the town. This route shares some of the features of the more advanced paddle, such as high cliffs and magnificent coastal views. But it is far less challenging – and attended by lifeguards.

11 STEER ALONG THE STOUR

A GENTLE, WILDLIFE-INFUSED PADDLE ALONG THE SHELTERED RIVER STOUR INTO CHRISTCHURCH HARBOUR

WHERE	River Stour, Christchurch, Dorset
STATS	←→ 13km (8 miles) return ①
START/FINISH	Iford Bridge ♀ SZ137935

There are a handful of different rivers called the Stour in Britain (all in England), but this River Stour winds 100km (60 miles) through the countryside of Wiltshire and Dorset. As the river journeys southwards, it encounters landscapes as varied as heathland, marshes and the chalk ridge of the Dorset Downs, eventually draining into the English Channel.

The low water levels of summer reveal diverse, botanically rich habitats along the river margin. These abound with colourful dragonflies and damselflies while different tones are provided by plants such as the appropriately vibrantly named purple loosestrife, whose impressive spikes are a magnet for butterflies, moths and bumblebees. Definitely worth keeping an eye out for.

Among birds, the usual suspects frolicking on the water include mallards, mute swans and moorhens. But also look (and listen) out for smaller species such as kingfishers (a strident cheeeek! heralds a glaucous-blue whirr of wings), sedge and reed warblers (brown birds chuntering noisily) and reed bunting (the

↑ The River Stour reaches the sea at Mudeford, at the eastern edge of Christchurch Harbour. (SS)

male with a black head and white moustache) that call the Stour home. It's also worth remembering to look up, as aerial interest includes birds of prey such as kestrel.

The other big (and I mean 'big') appeal of the Stour is its otter population. Just 40 years ago otters were on the verge of extinction across England, but clean-up initiatives have enabled otters to return to this stretch of waterway. While this exciting animal is normally tricky to spot given its unsocial hours (freshwater otters tend to be most active after dusk) and shy disposition, those of the Stour dispense with such etiquette and are regularly sighted splashing about unabashedly in broad daylight. Although sightings along this stretch are less frequent than the well-known (and comparatively extrovert) otters upstream at Blandford Forum, look for clues such as bubbles indicating an animal swimming underwater, a v-shaped furrow through the river or panicking ducks.

PADDLE THIS WAY

Launch next to the towpath downstream of Iford Bridge and take a moment to admire the stonework arches of the bridge itself. It dates back to the 12th century – possibly earlier.

Paddling downstream, you will notice a small caravan park on the left (east) which signals a bastion of the rural resisting the onwards march of urban Bournemouth that has already swallowed the area around your starting point at Iford Bridge. Don't expect true remoteness, however: there are more isolated and peaceful waterways in this book. Nevertheless, there's something to be said for the opportunity to peer (respectfully, without jeopardising the privacy of residents) at the perfectly manicured gardens and private moorings of *Grand Designs*-style properties gracing the edges of the Stour River.

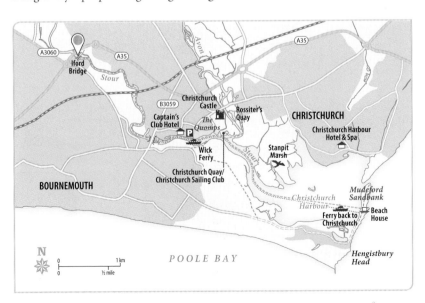

The river meanders peacefully for 3km (1¾ miles) through flat countryside with open fields separated by lines of trees, before gliding into the bustling seaside town of Christchurch, as signalled by the B3059 roadbridge. Fortunately, most of the town is set back from the Stour, so you won't be faced with too much brick.

That doesn't mean no people, however. Downstream from here, the Stour becomes a very busy stretch of water that is popular with boaters and paddlers, plus walkers along the towpaths and nearby Stour Valley Way (a major footpath). Many throng here because of the town's relaxed coastal vibe but also to take advantage of the sheltered waters. This calm stretch is perfect for novice paddlers to gain skills and build confidence before taking on more challenging routes.

Pass Wick Ferry, a rather grandly named passenger service crossing the river and departing from in front of the Captain's Club Hotel. Negotiate through numerous anchored boats, pass a park called The Quomps on your left (north) and a large open area to your right (south) to reach Christchurch Quay at Christchurch Sailing Club. There are usually hordes of mute swans round here, all looking to chaperone you past their territories or jostle you for food. I recommend avoiding eye contact and paddle past quickly to avoid aggravating them. (It's their waterway, after all.)

Just beyond Christchurch Quay the river forks, presenting you with two options. You could continue to Christchurch Harbour (perhaps to enjoy an afternoon picnic on the shores) before paddling up to the town itself to explore and people-watch or edge left towards the entrance to the River Avon. If you take the latter route, fork left quickly, pass Rossiter's Quay on your right (east) to reach the striking remains of Christchurch Castle, dating back to early AD1100, which drops straight into the water (in this case, a moat).

If you choose the former option, continue 2km downstream (past the shorebird-filled Stanpit Marsh nature reserve on your left, to the north) to enter Christchurch

GETTING THERE

Iford Bridge, on Old Bridge Road, lies on the northern outskirts of Christchurch, just northeast of the A3060/A35 roundabout. There is limited roadside parking in Iford Bridge; I recommend arriving early to nab a space. Nearest train station is Christchurch, from where you can take bus 1a to Iford Bridge.

HIRE & LESSONS

South Coast Canoes (south-coast-canoes.co.uk) offers guided tours and canoe equipment hire. Shore Sports based in Christchurch Harbour (shoresports. co.uk), offers hire, tours and lessons for kayak and SUP.

→ In summer, look for sedge warblers singing from riverside vegetation. (James Lowen)

Harbour. Then head east for just over 1km (²/₃ mile), making a beeline for the spit directly ahead that separates the harbour from the sea.

The closer you get, the sweeter the sight of Mudeford Sandbank becomes. Rows of impeccable wooden-panelled beach huts, painted in an assortment of pastel shades, come into focus. It is not for nothing that Christchurch is renowned for its seaside charm. On the sandy spit, snuggled amid the huts, sits a small, glass-fronted café called Beach House. From within a blue and white interior, fantastic views are complemented by delicious seafood. So why not moor up and enjoy a glass of something cold to boot.

For the return journey you can jump on a boat (⬦ bournemouthboating.co.uk) running from Mudeford Sandbank to Christchurch Quay then paddle the short distance upstream to Iford Bridge. Alternatively, if you prefer a more demanding day out, retrace the entire route by board.

WHERE TO STAY & EAT

The Beach House (⬦ beachhousecafe.co.uk) sits on the spit at Mudeford Sandbank and affords magnificent views west across Christchurch Harbour and south to Hengistbury Head. If you want something a little more luxurious, Christchurch Harbour Hotel and Spa (⬦ christchurch-harbour-hotel.co.uk) is a waterfront venue that offers a bar, restaurant, overnight accommodation and pampering. Perfect for unwinding after a paddle.

TITBITS

Be aware that the narrow entrance in and out of the harbour (ie: at the east, by Mudeford Sandbank) can create a very strong tidal flow.

↑ The River Stour passes the town of Christchurch on its route eastwards. (Mike Charles/S)

12 MEET THE MEANDERS

WIND ALONG THE CUCKMERE RIVER TO THE SEA, THE SPECTACULAR SEVEN SISTERS CLIFFS AT YOUR SHOULDER

WHERE	Cuckmere River, East Sussex
STATS	←→ 6km (4 miles) plus optional extension of 5km (3 miles), both return
	① – ③ (for extended route)
START/FINISH	Cuckmere Valley Canoe Club slipway ⑨ TV518993

I t is believed that the name Cuckmere derives from an Old English word meaning 'fast flowing'. Given the River Cuckmere's steep descent of more than 100m in its initial 6km (4 miles), this is both perfectly plausible and a fitting tribute. On the assumption that you are not a fearless thrill-seeker, you'll be relieved to learn that this route – at the very end of the river's course in the heart of Sussex's Seven Sisters Country Park (🌿 sevensisters.org.uk) – is not all a white-knuckle ride. A section of non-tidal waters here is just the ticket for those who prefer calmer paddles.

In 1847, a straight cut was added to the Cuckmere River, creating two separate channels. The new section diverted any flow from the meanders and instead sent water straight down the river. This ultimately protected the river from the force of the sea. The resulting verdant floodplain, with steep chalk downland rising to the east, is that happy by-product: the perfect spot for a gentle paddle.

Adrenaline junkies can warm up here then head for a feistier adventure on the tidal stretch of the Cuckmere – the river mouth, where fresh water greets the salty sea at Cuckmere Haven. Here you'll witness the famous Seven Sisters – an astonishing series of domineering chalk cliffs stretching towards 100m high. These culminate in Britain's highest coastal cliff made of the white stuff – Beachy Head,

↑ Cuckmere River meanders generously before greeting the English Channel at Cuckmere Haven. (Sam Moore/SDNPA)

at 162m above sea level. (If you don't get a cricked neck looking up at Seven Sisters, paddling on to Beachy Head ought to do the trick!)

The route flows through the Cuckmere Valley, a Site of Special Scientific Interest (SSSI), and that is also part of the South Downs National Park. Given it's a nature reserve there are some wildlife highlights that you can look out for too. Little egrets and lapwings are year-round residents, while wildfowl and wigeon make the area home for winter. There's even more variety down at Cuckmere Haven, including common lizard, chalkhill blue butterflies and green winged orchid on the chalk grassland.

This short route is perfect for beginners and, dare I say, is even a little romantic – should you be looking for something that makes an

impression. Watching the sun set while savouring an alfresco picnic on a quiet summer's evening is one of life's pleasures. Simple, but wonderful.

PADDLE THIS WAY

Launch from the public slipway at Seven Sisters Country Park. Heading down the eastern branch of the Cuckmere River, glide straight into 3km of wide meanders through the lower floodplain. This journey is all about kicking back and enjoying the countryside that envelops this winding paddle unique for its natural river meanders without any tidal force.

The short route stops as you become hemmed in by banks and can proceed no further. If, however, you are an experienced paddler or one looking for something

↑ Taking a well-earned breather at Seven Sisters. (Gareth McCormack/Alamy)

more daring then it's time for a punchy addition to the route. Instead of returning north, pull out on the bank and lug your board over the pathway to the west to reach the tidal part of the Cuckmere River. (Take care here, as the terrain can be slippery and/or muddy.)

The experience now could not be more different. The paddle downstream lives up to the Cuckmere's etymology. Whizzing along 1km (⅔ mile) of fast-flowing tidal river, you soon reach the mouth of the river, feeding the English Channel. This is Cuckmere Haven, a well-known spot for wildlife-watching.

As you enter the mini-estuary, take a left and follow the cliff edge east for around 500m (⅓ mile) until you are flanked by the dramatic and eye-searingly white Seven Sisters chalk cliffs. Paddle east for a further 2km (1¼ miles) beneath this magnificent structure. The sheer drop into the water is an undeniably dramatic sight – but also not without danger. Falling rock is not uncommon, so I suggest admiring from a safe distance, staying at least 10m back at high tide.

It is fair to say that these towering cliffs are one landmark you cannot possibly miss. When you have had your fill, return the way you came.

GETTING THERE

From the A259 3km (2 miles) east of Seaford, turn south at the Seven Sisters Country Park visitor centre (⊘ sevensisters.org.uk) at Exceat. Use the car park next to the slipway by Cuckmere Valley Canoe Club (⊘ cvcc.org.uk). The waterway is protected, and this is the only legitimate entry point on to the meanders. Nearest train station is Seaford, from where you can take bus 12, 12A or 13 to the Country Park (⊘ sevensisters.org.uk/page4.html).

HIRE & LESSONS

Buzz Active Cuckmere (⊘ buzzactive.co.uk) is co-located with the Cuckmere Valley Canoe Club and rents boards for use on the meanders. If, however, you plan to continue down the tidal river, you will require your own equipment.

WHEN TO GO

The meanders are particularly beautiful at sunset, or by moonlight. (Don't try the wilder section at night, however.)

WHERE TO STAY & EAT

The Country Park runs the Saltmarsh Café (⊘ saltmarshfarmhouse.co.uk) in Exceat. You can also stay here, or at the Country Park's Foxhole Campsite (⊘ sevensisters.org.uk/wheretostay.html). In Seaford, The Wellington (⊘ thewellington-hotel.com) is a decent pub-with-rooms and serves good-quality traditional grub.

13 BALLET OF THE STARLINGS

TAKE TO THE WATER FOR A NOVEL PERSPECTIVE ON BRIGHTON'S MESMERISING MURMURATION

WHERE	Brighton Pier, East Sussex
STATS	↔ up to 10.5km (6½ miles) return ① – ②
START/FINISH	Brighton Beach ♀ TQ315037

Brighton seafront offers everything expected of an English seaside resort. There is a pebble beach, a pier, a helter-skelter ride; amusement arcades and – of course – fish and chips. But are you aware of Brighton's most spectacular (and entirely natural) performance?

Taking place on many evenings from late autumn until late winter, the 'murmuration' of starlings is an aerial ballet, as thousands of birds fly in synchrony – twisting and turning, rising and falling – before the birds drop to roost. The spectacle can be viewed from anywhere along the seafront and while, sadly, numbers appear to be in decline, it remains a sight to behold. Most people-watch from the beach, but my recommendation is to escape the human hustle and bustle by taking your board a few score metres out into the English Channel. Here your only company will be the protagonists, and the only sounds the whooshing of their wings and the whispering of the waves.

So that's Brighton paddled by night (well, in the evening), but what about by day? It would be rude not to take advantage of paddling parallel with Brighton's 8km (5 miles) of shingle beach, with striking features such as the sadly abandoned West Pier.

↑ Paddle offshore and you will have the best 'seat' at starling showtime. (David Rice/A)

PADDLE THIS WAY

Launch from the shores of Brighton's pebbly beach, east of the famous Palace Pier. As you push away from the beach, head south and then either paddle underneath the pier (eavesdropping on the excited chatter of tourists) or curve south around it. Then turn west towards Hove and continue parallel with the

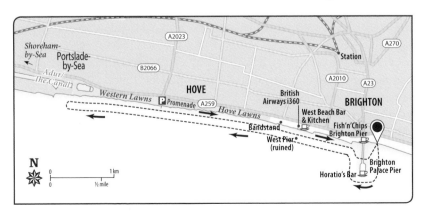

beach. Stay equidistant with the pier or, if you fancy some people-watching, head closer to the beach (and the seafront promenade).

After 1.2km (¾ mile), you will reach the majestic-yet-sad skeleton that was once Brighton's West Pier – the first in Britain to be listed as a Grade-1-listed building. Of course, this can be admired from some distance – but there's something to be said for using your board to get up close and moseying around the remnants.

On the shore parallel with West Pier is a striking, sizeable and evidently contemporary needle-shaped structure with what appears to be a circular doughnut moving up and down its shaft. Designed by the people behind the London Eye, the British Airways i360 offers panoramic views across Brighton, the South Downs and even the Isle of Wight on clear days, all from the top of its 138m-high observation platform.

Some 300m further west is the historic seafront bandstand, restored in a fashion sympathetic to the charm of its original Victorian era. Overlooking the beach, the structure marks the transition from Brighton to Hove.

↑ To see starlings perform at Brighton, time your visit for a sunny evening in autumn or winter. (Neil Irwin)

Continue west towards Portslade-by-Sea and you will notice the beach and promenade become quieter and a more residential setting with 2km (1¼ miles) worth of flat green lawns replacing beachside buildings. Some 4km (2½ miles) west of West Pier, all changes again as the coast becomes industrialised as far as the River Adur at Shoreham-by-Sea. The River Adur is a firm favourite of paddlers (see *Titbits* below) but the intervening deterioration in views suggests that many of you will prefer to turn back east and return to the beach beyond Palace Pier. After all, there's the pebbly beach and fish and chips to enjoy…

GETTING THERE

Access is straightforward. The A259 runs along the Brighton seafront, and there's parking available along the promenade. (Note that this can get busy, particularly in summer or on sunny days, so it is best to arrive early.) Nearest train station is Brighton, from where it is a 1.5km (1 mile) walk to Brighton Palace Pier. Launch from the beach just east of the pier.

HIRE & LESSONS

Brighton Kitesurf and SUP Academy (⊘ brightonkitesurfandsupacademy.com) offers lessons.

WHEN TO GO

If you want to witness the starling murmurations then winter evenings between November and early March offer the best chance. (Nothing is guaranteed, however.) To maximise your chances, ensure that you are on the water about an hour before dusk. The ballet may be performed anywhere between the two piers. Murmurations tend to be more impressive on clear, still evenings.

WHERE TO STAY & EAT

Brighton brims with accommodation options and places to eat. One personal favourite is Horatio's Bar (⊘ brightonpier.co.uk/eat-and-drink/horatios-bar), an old-fashioned bar at the end of Brighton Pier. The views are excellent. Further along the coast, I also like the relaxed setting and traditional seaside fare served by West Beach Bar & Kitchen (⊘ westbeachbarandkitchen.com), situated under the British Airways i360 tower (⊘ britishairwaysi360.com). If it's fresh marine produce you're after then Fish'n'Chips Brighton Pier (⊘ brightonpier.co.uk) is a must; I particularly like the cockles.

TITBITS

Beware of the conditions. A helpful tailwind turns into a headwind on your return. A still day is ideal. If it is too breezy, paddle with the wind behind you then walk along the promenade (or catch bus 1/1A or a taxi) back to the start. The River Adur – starting at Shoreham-by-Sea – is a very popular area for paddlers; being 30-odd kilometres (20 miles) long, it would make for a great weekend adventure. Paddleboarders, canoeists and kayakers unite for the yearly Paddle Round the Pier (⊘ paddleroundthepier.com) on Hove Lawns.

14 BEAULIEU BEAUTY

EXPLORE A DIFFERENT SIDE OF THE NEW FOREST BY PADDLING THROUGH A RIVERINE NATURE RESERVE

WHERE	River Beaulieu, New Forest, Hampshire
STATS	←→ 16km (10 miles) return ②
START/FINISH	Buckler's Hard quay ♀ SU409001

'**B**eaulieu' (pronounced 'bew-lee') is French for 'beautiful place' – which is the first clue as to what you can expect from the river of the same name that meanders for 19km (12 miles) through the southeastern section of Hampshire's New Forest. Downstream of Beaulieu village, the river is generously fringed by North Solent nature reserve. This protected area covers a whopping 820ha of attractive shingle banks, saltmarsh, woodland, heathland and grassland. Although not all these landscapes are visible from the paddle route, it's still quite some habitat diversity in a single place – so, unsurprisingly, you can expect to see some interesting wildlife from the water. Look for curlews, redshanks and oystercatchers, for example, feeding on the mud.

Historical interest complements this natural appeal. Buckler's Hard is now a sleepy, pretty hamlet with Georgian homes leading down to the water. In the 18th century, however, it was a shipbuilding centre, even providing vessels for the Royal Navy commanded by Admiral Horatio Lord Nelson. Nowadays the hamlet's maritime museum (⌂ bucklershard.co.uk) offers reconstructions of what life was like then.

In the village of Beaulieu, meanwhile, an attractive millpond, Palace House and Abbey ruins are dotted around the shores of the River Beaulieu. Everything about this village is steeped in historic country charm; there are small stone cottages, flat rolling fields, farmland and small independent shops lining the narrow streets. Bucolic Britain at its best.

↑ Yachts are the modern legacy of the shipbuilding heyday of Buckler's Hard. (BBA Photography/S)

PADDLE THIS WAY

Having paid your paddling fee (see *Titbits*, page 79), launch from the pontoon at Buckler's Hard quay. The marina here was built in the 18th century to serve the West Indian sugar trade. Sailboats on stilts flank the waterway, and the harbour bobs with boats that require weaving between, especially in summer.

As you paddle north, past a meander, you'll soon see the thatched roof of Duke's Bath Cottage. This was built by George, the first Duke of Montagu, in 1790 to help him with his arthritis. As salt was considered to alleviate suffering, the duke's garden pond was linked to the river and transformed into a saltwater bathing spot.

There is more striking visual evidence of this salinity as you continue north. Around the water is a vast, flat expanse of bare land. This is a result of 'salting', whereby a combination of saline waters and poor drainage stunt the growth of any trees that try to root at the river's edge.

Continuing, you pass small creeks and indents that create the perfect conditions for the growth of plumed reeds. While these all add to create an idyllic river scene, take care. If you choose to explore these nooks and crannies, be careful of catching your fin – a problem I experience frequently on quieter waterways.

Next you will come to two ancient woodlots – first Burnt Oak Copse, then Keeping Copse – on the river's southern shore. These adjacent wooded pastures

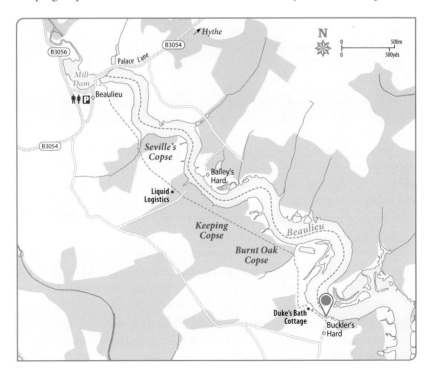

provide a real connection to the forest, despite you being on the water. Continue north, rounding two meanders. Continuing broadly northwest as the river twists and turns through fine Hampshire countryside, including grassland and saltmarsh, you will spot Bailey's Hard. This is a significant maritime landmark, once being used for shipbuilding. HMS *Salisbury*, the very first naval vessel to be built on the Beaulieu, was completed here in 1698.

By now the paddle may be getting rather tough, but the thicket of Seville's Copse on the south shore is a sure sign that you are nearing the turnaround point. Indeed, the village of Beaulieu soon comes into view and, beyond it, Mill Dam, which powered Beaulieu's tidal mill until 1945.

Talking of hydro-power, now that you have reached the midpoint of the route, it is time to take advantage of it. Given that breaking the journey by getting out on the riverbanks is not permitted here, simply turn round so you are facing

↑ Ponies are an integral feature in the New Forest landscape. (Michael Dedman/S)

downstream… and literally go with the flow. It may be 8km (5 miles) away, but – as long as there is no headwind – the end of the paddle (back at Buckler's Hard) comes upon you surprisingly quickly. Were you to continue downstream, you'd reach the Solent and then Cowes on the Isle of Wight.

Once ashore, you're due a treat. Follow the short walkway from the pontoon and a small ice-cream shack stares you in the face. If that's not a sign from above then what is? Or perhaps you are after something a little stronger? If so, take a left at the pontoon and ascend a short, grassy incline. The red doorway on the right with the picnic tables outside is, in fact, a little pub called The Master Builder's. Whichever you choose, you've earnt it.

GETTING THERE

From junction 2 of the M27, follow the A326 southeast to Hythe, where you turn southwest on the B3056 to Beaulieu village. Just south of Beaulieu village turn left (south) along a minor road for 3km (1¾ miles) to reach Buckler's Hard. Use the car park (SZ409998). Nearest train station is Beaulieu Road 8km (5 miles) north, from where you will need to take a taxi, although there are more regular services to Brockenhurst 10km (6 miles) west, from where you can take bus 483.

HIRE & LESSONS

Liquid Logistics (liquidlogistics.co.uk), just south of Beaulieu, offers instructor-led paddling trips, as well as renting canoes and kayaks (but not paddleboards).

WHERE TO STAY & EAT

Captain's Cabin Tea Rooms at Buckler's Hard (bucklershard.co.uk/tea-rooms/) is 200m uphill from the pontoon and has an outdoor seating area that is ideal for long summer days. En route is The Master Builder's pub (hillbrookehotels.co.uk/the-master-builders/), which also has rooms. I can also recommend the very small ice-cream shack as you come off the pontoon. At Beaulieu Road train station, Beaulieu Hotel (newforesthotels.co.uk/beaulieu-hotel/) is a good option for overnight accommodation; an adjacent pub serves food.

TITBITS

There are a few important points to note. First, the Beaulieu River and its banks are privately owned by Lord Montagu, so you need to buy a £5 permit from Beaulieu Estate Office (01590 614621; estate@beaulieu.co.uk) before you can paddle. You also need to stay on the water, rather than coming to shore in Beaulieu, for example. Second, this return journey is fine on a still day. With a headwind in either direction, it will be tiring on a paddleboard (less so in a kayak or canoe). Moreover, strong tides can make for hazardous paddling for the inexperienced. Finally, it is also worth noting that the number of sailing boats in Buckler's Hard means that it can be busy.

15 WEY TO GO

TRY A COMMUTE WITH A DIFFERENCE, PADDLING THROUGH SURREY'S STOCKBROKER BELT TOWARDS THE THAMES

WHERE	River Wey, Surrey/London
STATS	↔ 23km (14 miles) ⏳ 1–2 days ①
START	Catteshall Lock, Godalming ♥ SU980445
FINISH	Thames Lock, Weybridge ♥ TQ072655

From as early as the 17th century the River Wey had been adapted for commercial use and was the lifeblood of London. It provided an arterial route for commerce to and from the capital and sustained the livelihoods of communities lining its banks. In its heyday, this rural navigation was a hive of activity. Horse-drawn barges pulled cargo along the water; this was a money-making operation that ran with military precision, albeit one dictated by the tides of the Thames.

The Wey Navigation stopped operations in the early 1960s and, subsequently, the pace has slowed significantly – with the key use becoming recreation. The Navigation has become a bucolic waterway popular with paddlers, punters, canal boaters and walkers. All come to enjoy wide, green landscapes, their escape facilitated by easy access from the capital or Surrey's commuter belt.

↑ Coxes Mill and Lock on the River Wey near Addlestone. (Paul Daniels/S)

Follow the water from Godalming to Thames Lock, however, and you will encounter ample signs of the Wey's vibrant, industrial past. The banks are dusted with disused mills, long-established churches and even the remains of castles. How things have changed!

PADDLE THIS WAY

Launch on to the Wey next to the bridge at Catteshall Lock, and head northeast towards Guildford, 10km (6¼ miles) downstream. The fields that line the waters here impart an immediate tranquillity that sets the tone for this paddle. Glide downstream for 2km (1¼ miles) until you reach the first lock by an industrial estate at Peasmarsh. Portage around it and continue under a small footbridge then beneath the A248 bridge and a small weir on the right (east).

As you paddle, take in the leafy trees lining the riverbanks, all perfectly reflected in the mirror-like water. This is a particularly rural section where it is not unusual to spot roe deer grazing in waterside fields. Look up to see birds such as kestrels and – if you stay out until dusk – watch Daubenton's bats zipping over the water as they hunt tiny winged insects. That said, this route isn't one best enjoyed in the dark.

Beyond here, just before Broadford, you'll reach a fork on the river. Keep left to continue along the Navigation and watch the landscape transform. Admittedly, the short stretch past a large riverside car park and industrial structures is a bit of an eyesore compared with the start of the route. But this temporary ugliness makes the return to open countryside – once you've paddled under another roadbridge, weir and railway line – all the sweeter.

About 500m (⅓ mile) beyond the railway line, you reach St Catherine's Lock on the left. This requires a brief portage. Once back on the river, meander through leafy countryside before descending into Guildford with its waterside theatre, bars and restaurants. This stretch of river is favoured by walkers and rowers. (Keep an eye out for the latter as they face backwards so unless there's a cox the chances of them seeing you are slim.)

Once past Guildford, paddle under the A3 and then proceed roughly parallel with it for 5km (3 miles), before you veer left when the river forks again, away from the noise of the traffic. Although the landscape is pastoral, noise from the dual carriageway can slightly interfere with the more pleasant hum of nature (nothing beats birdsong!). But even this minimal assault on the senses means that it is a relief when you pull away perpendicular to the A3. You'll soon reach Triggs Lock, usually heralded by a long line of moored canal boats. Turn right immediately after the lock.

A further 1km (⅔ mile) downstream, a smattering of houses forms the prelude to a fork, where you bear right (northeast), keeping the towpath to your right. Soon you will arrive in the village of Send where you'll see a waterside pub, The New Inn. Continue for another 2km (1¼ miles) to Papercourt Lock until you reach

another fork. Bear right here (under the B367) and continue to a weir. Keep left, passing under a small footbridge. Here the river becomes shrouded by tall trees; forsake views and welcome the seclusion. Left (west) of the towpath, look for a small summerhouse. This provided haven for the illustrious poet, John Donne, who penned some of his most famous works from here.

Once under the M25, you are on the final stretch of the paddle – a leg of 4.5km (2¾ miles) to reach Thames Lock, where the Wey greets the Thames on the latter's journey east into London. Much of this route remains flanked by trees, as if stubbornly resisting London's imminence. On the very final stretch trees are replaced by manicured lawns of the 'millionaire mansions' for which this area is renowned. A garden makeover by TV's *Ground Force* might provide a bit more scenic variety here… Pull up when you reach Thames Lock and haul out, mission complete.

↑ Towpath between the River Wey and the Wey Navigation. (thatmacroguy/S)

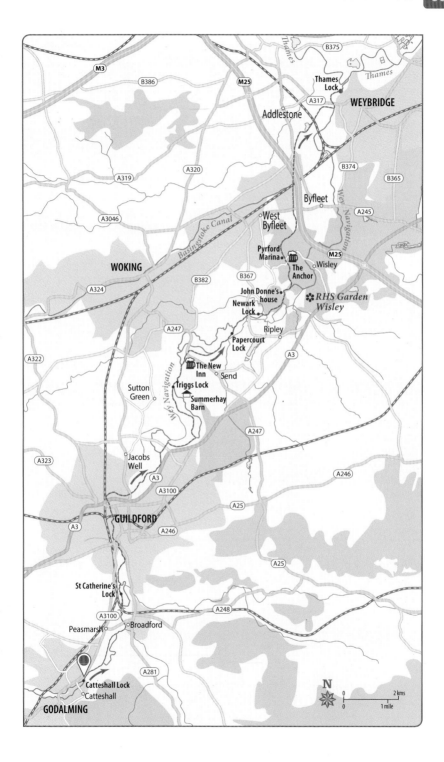

GETTING THERE

From Godalming take the A3100 northeast towards Guildford. Turn on to Catteshall Road and park on the roadside near the bridge. Launch from beneath the adjacent lock. Nearest train station is Godalming, from where it is a 2km (1¼ mile) walk to the start point.

HIRE & LESSONS

You will need your own equipment, as there is no hire available along the Navigation.

WHERE TO STAY & EAT

Nestled on the banks of the Wey in Send sits an 18th-century pub, The New Inn (thenewinnsend.com), which is popular with boaters, locals and fishermen. At Pyrford Marina, about 2km (1¼ miles) shy of the M25, The Anchor (anchorpyrford.co.uk) is a traditional English country pub conveniently situated on the banks of the Wey, with an enticing riverside terrace. If you plan a two-day trip, the limited overnight accommodation options include Sommerhay Barn near Send (sommerhaybarn.co.uk) and The Queen's Head pub in Byfleet (queensheadbyfleet.co.uk). Both are a (short) walk from the river, so it may be wise to consider wild camping (page 11).

TITBITS

This route, while long, can be completed in a single day provided you've got a tailwind to propel you. Head- or crosswinds will slow progress considerably, which might make it worth shortening the route or finding somewhere to stop overnight before finishing the second leg the following day. Whatever you do, don't rush – this route should be taken slowly, to absorb the surprising beauty of your commuter-belt surroundings.

Lizzie and friend paddling through the calm waters of the Wey Navigation. (Neil Irwin)

16 PADDLE FIT FOR A KING?

DRIFT ALONG BRITAIN'S MOST FAMOUS RIVER AS IT FLOWS TOWARDS CENTRAL LONDON

WHERE	Kingston-upon-Thames, London
STATS	←→ 15km (9⅓ miles) return ②
START/FINISH	Kingston Quay 📍 TQ177692

This book could not possibly be complete without at least a gentle nod to one of the world's most famous rivers right here in Britain – the Thames. Along its course of 345km (215 miles), the River Thames meanders through some of England's most historically, culturally and architecturally significant sites, and has been a crucial trade thoroughfare throughout British history. A book on paddling without a route along this waterway is simply unthinkable.

Indeed, what would London have been without the Thames? What is now a multi-cultural metropolis was first and foremost a port, developed as such by the Romans who settled on a site named Londinium – right beside the River Thames. Later the Saxons, the Normans and the Tudors all benefited Londonium's status as a centre for trading and shipbuilding.

But which section of the Thames should one paddle? I favour the stretch between Kingston and Richmond, upstream from the city. This brings a wealth of interesting, significant landmarks and scenery. Moreover, the route is far enough from the chaos of the city to enable you to feel that you have escaped, yet close enough to make it easily accessible for those coming from (or via) the capital.

↑ Life at Richmond-on-Thames revolves around Britain's most famous river. (asiastock/S)

In historical terms, Kingston itself is notable. Saxon kings were crowned here, and the name Kingston derives from the Old English for 'the King's estate'. Moreover, Kingston Bridge was only the Thames's second crossing point, after London Bridge. Meanwhile, Richmond, the end point of the paddle, is known for its famous Royal Park. The area around Richmond Bridge has been redeveloped in recent years so that plenty of eateries complement the existing green space. The result is a lively outdoor area for people to enjoy in the warmer months – and the perfect place to refuel before returning to Kingston.

PADDLE THIS WAY

Head off from the steps just downstream of Kingston Bridge and

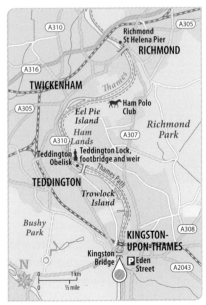

turn right (north) to paddle under the bridge. Go under the railway bridge then keep left of a small island mid-river. Using the bridges and islands along this route is a helpful way of maintaining your bearings. This area is highly residential, with rows of houses and moorings lining the river.

As you enter Teddington, roughly 2km (1¼ miles) from the start, you will pass another island – Trowlock, which is long, slender and residential, and lies parallel

↑ Paddlers are not the only people to take to the water at Richmond-on-Thames. (SS)

with the riverbank. Continue a further 500m (⅓ mile) to approach Teddington Lock and weir. Look out for Egyptian goose (not native but now unequivocally part of London waterways), grey heron, mute swans and kingfisher.

Pass Teddington Obelisk on your right (east) and sweep right alongside the wooded park of Ham Lands. The descent into Twickenham will be marked by – you guessed it – another island. Its name, Eel Pie, comes from the aquatic food served from a small inn here during the 19th century. The greenness continues on both sides – not bad for a capital city, is it? – and includes Ham Polo Club to your right (south). As you approach Richmond you'll pass under the wide roadbridge that leads to the redeveloped and pedestrianised area of the town. Pull up at the slipway by The White Cross pub and get yourself a drink, or head ashore at Richmond St Helena Pier (a pontoon) by a small park and relax. When you're ready, paddle back to the start.

GETTING THERE

Launch from the Thames Path (riverside walk) between the A307 (which runs along the eastern bank of the River Thames) at Kingston Bridge. Nearest parking is at Eden Street car park. Nearest train stations are Hampton Wick or Kingston, which both lie on routes to/from several London stations.

HIRE & LESSONS

Richmond-based Back of Beyond (⊘ backofbeyonduk.com) runs SUP and kayaking lessons as well as socials and wild camps via canoe, SUP and kayak.

WHERE TO STAY & EAT

The small riverside pub, The White Cross (⊘ thewhitecrossrichmond.com), is right next to the slipway that marks the turnaround point in Richmond.

TITBITS

Three words of warning. There may be boaters and rowers at any point along this route, but particularly around Kingston and Twickenham, respectively. Boaters will likely pass quicker than you can paddle. Once when I paddled here, some disrespectful individuals even deliberately created a wake to make it harder for me to paddle. It's the first and only time that's ever happened to me, but worth sharing so you are aware. In terms of rowers, remember that most boats lack a cox and can't see where they are going. Accordingly, it's your responsibility to dodge away from them, or yell far enough in advance for them to change course. Finally, check tides on the Port of London Authority website (⊘ pla.co.uk). For a shorter version of this route or if travelling by car, then you can launch from River Lane in Petersham (free, roadside parking by the slipway) and either head upstream towards Twickenham and Kingston or downsteam towards Richmond.

17 A TRIP TO PADDLINGTON

ESCAPE THE CONCRETE JUNGLE
WITHOUT LEAVING LONDON

WHERE	Regent's Canal, London
STATS	↔ 7km (4⅓ miles) return ①
START/FINISH	Paddington Basin, North Wharf Road ⚲ TQ268815

This is a capital paddle indeed: a classy urban journey through the heart of London along a historic and atmospheric waterway. I have great personal affection for the eight-mile-long, characterful Regent's Canal: it was both the very first place I paddled in London and where Plastic Patrol was born. While most of my exploration has been about landscape and wildlife, Regent's Canal offers something totally different – a paddle like no other. And so it should: we're in inner-city London, after all.

My suggested route isn't too long, which makes it more about enjoyment than endurance. It enables you to experience this diverse metropolis in an entirely novel way. Paddling through London should feel hectic but isn't. There's enough life and buzz to enthral, but being on the water pleasurably muffles any excess sound, thus making for a surprisingly restful paddle.

↑ London's waterborne homes: narrowboats line Regent's Canal near Little Venice. (SS)

PADDLE THIS WAY

Start on the north bank of Paddington Basin outside a little café called KUPP and opposite St Mary's Hospital. Being partly enclosed, there is no through traffic here, so it's the perfect place for beginners to develop technique and confidence before paddling northwest along Regent's Canal towards Little Venice.

Travel for just under 1km (⅔ mile), underneath the noisy A40 Westway flyover, to where the canal narrows under a bridge (so narrow indeed, that only one boat can pass through at a time). Here you will notice an island amid a much more open expanse of water. This marks Little Venice, part of the wider Maida Vale area. It's surprisingly tranquil with painted houseboats and barges that could belong on a postcard. Paddle around the island, admiring – from a respectful distance – the mute swans that breed there.

The stretch of water either side of Little Venice dissects an affluent area and is bordered by trendy waterside bars and restaurants. Its proximity to Paddington train station means the towpaths are always buzzing with people so there's plenty to keep you entertained. Regent's Canal offers a candid snapshot of the diversification of London and gifts a paddling adventure like no other.

There are two exits from Little Venice. Ignore the one to the right (northeast) which heads alongside Maida Avenue towards Regent's Park and Camden; a long tunnel along here restricts access for paddlers. Instead, head left. As you do so, you pass underneath a blue bridge where you will doubtless attract the attention of passers-by, hopefully intrigued by those who think differently enough to explore London from the waterway.

Keep paddling along the canal in a broadly northwesterly direction, heading towards Kensal Town. (Stay mindful of boaters as this area can get busy.) After about 2km (1¼ miles), you will see The Union Tavern pub with its brightly painted tables and sheltered outdoor area. Indulge in a spot of people-watching as you

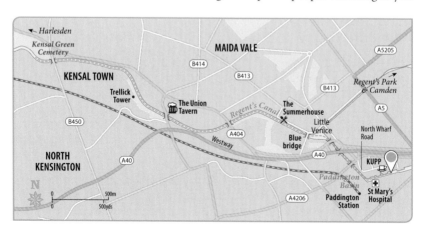

glide past. Sadly, serrated black railings lining the water's edge prevent you from mooring up for a bit to eat – but fret not, as there are plenty of other food and drink options along the way.

About 200m beyond the pub, the heights of Trellick Tower dominate the view to your left, slightly back from the west bank. This block of flats, designed by Ernō Goldfinger and opened in 1972, is an exemplar of what is known as 'Brutalist' architecture. Although listed, this building ferociously divides opinions. You either love it or hate it; there's no middle ground. This is London at its edgiest.

Continue northwest and you'll reach inner Kensal Town and eventually Harlesden. These heavily redeveloped areas are a far cry from their 1930s selves. Harlesden epitomises the diversity for which London is justly recognised. In 2015, it suffered more gun-crime than anywhere else in the capital. Yet by 2017, house prices were rising faster here than any other London borough. It seems the only thing that stays the same in London is its canal. Once you have finished exploring Harlesden, perhaps around Kensal Green Cemetery, simply turn round and head back southeast for 3.5km (2¼ miles) along Regent's Canal back to Paddington Basin.

GETTING THERE

Access to Paddington Basin is off North Wharf Road, itself off the A4206 and A40 Westway. Park at Paddington train station. The nearest station on the London Underground is Edgware Road, and the nearest train station is Paddington. Public transport is clearly fine for inflatable boards, but not rigid ones.

HIRE & LESSONS

You can hire equipment and kit or book lessons and guided tours through London-based provider Active 360 (⬦ active360.co.uk/paddleboarding-paddington.htm).

WHERE TO STAY & EAT

On Paddington Basin, Nordic-inspired café KUPP (⬦ kupp.co/locations/paddington/) does a great coffee and posh hot dogs if you want a snack before you set off. There are other pubs and bars dotted along the waterway throughout your paddle too. The Summerhouse serves up delicious seafood and overlooks the canal (⬦ thesummerhouse.co). Convenient accommodation hotels include Novotel London Paddington (⬦ tinyurl.com/novotel-paddle), a few minutes' walk from Paddington Basin.

TITBITS

Regent's Canal is 'home' to me when I paddleboard but its inner-city location means that it accumulates plastic. It was a coot's nest here, almost entirely constructed from plastic, that inspired the start of my campaigning and my decision to paddle the length of England.

↑ Paddling the Regent's Canal through Little Venice. (active360.co.uk)

18 RUMBLE IN THE MUMBLES

PADDLE PAST THE MUMBLES ON THIS CONSUMMATE WELSH SEASIDE PADDLE

WHERE	The Mumbles, Swansea
STATS	←→ 3km (2 miles) return ②
START/FINISH	Slipway, The Mumbles ♀ SS623877

The Mumbles marks the segue from Swansea Bay to the coastline that extends westwards to form the Gower Peninsula, possibly the most beautiful lowland region in Wales. Flanked alternately by steep, craggy cliffs and expansive hills, The Mumbles's traditional British seaside charm – including a long seafront promenade and delightful pier – seduced the likes of Dylan Thomas (born nearby in Swansea). Indeed, it continues to enchant numerous tourists smitten by a unique area of the Welsh coast that remains steeped in tradition.

The Mumbles's most iconic feature – indeed, its focal point – is its pier built in 1898 (although closed for restoration at the time of writing). That said, it's arguably a close-run contest with the lighthouse that sits on a small island just east of the pier. This was built in 1794 in order to guide vessels into the thriving port of Swansea. Now redundant, its primary purpose now seems to be as a photographic subject.

Waters here are typically calm because The Mumbles's seafront is sheltered by the peninsula that runs from Mumbles Hill southeast to terminate in Mumbles Head – a steep and dramatic frontage compared with the flatter, more open countryside at the other side of the bay. This protection means that novice paddlers looking for an open-water adventure can get stuck right in. So what are you waiting for?

PADDLE THIS WAY

Slightly east of the midway point along the coast road, about 800m (½ mile) west of Mumbles Pier, take your board, canoe or kayak to the concrete slipway that slopes into the water. Before getting into the water, peruse the vista.

Look left (northwest) and, in the distance, you'll see small mounds toned yellow, brown or green. Before letting your eyes be swept up by the rolling countryside,

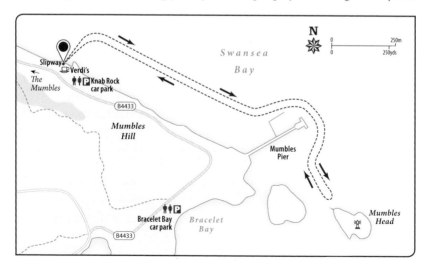

← The iconic pier at The Mumbles dominates this coastal route. (BrianOrman/S)

focus on the foreground, where you'll see white squares of houses whose residents enjoy a picture-perfect view over The Mumbles or the water – or, in some cases, both! Look right (eastsoutheast) and you'll see the town's traditional seaside pier. According to a sign near its entrance, it would take a typical snail 53 hours to journey to the end of the pier. To the south of the pier, two rocky islands break off Mumbles Head, the outermost of which is topped by the lighthouse. Finally, look directly ahead (northeast), noticing boats strewn across the shallows, which cede to blue water beyond which lurks the silhouette of Swansea, which stays a respectful distance away.

Paddle right (east) towards the pier, taking a moment to listen to the gulls circling above as you approach. The birds' strident calls are not the only noise reaching your ears as you dip paddle in water. The murmur of chatter will also start to rise as you glide under the wooden base of the pier. Peer up through the cracks in the old wooden panels and you may spot passers-by in mid-stroll. At

↑ Lizzie paddling on a serene Swansea Bay at The Mumbles. (Lizzie Carr)

this moment, your position is gloriously privileged: close enough to sense the holidaymakers' buzz yet sufficiently distant to feel separate from the tourist bustle.

Continue to paddle broadly eastwards, breaking away from the pier towards the two small islands beyond Mumbles Head. Approach the second island to take a close look at its lighthouse. If you're paddling during the evening and the sky is clear, try and stay out until sunset and watch the red orb slowly fall behind the island. Then paddle back west, roughly retracing your route to the slipway, under pastel-pink skies.

By now, any crowds on the pier will have dissipated. That might encourage you to venture there yourself. If so, pull into the small sandy bay that overlooks both the pier and the islands. Walk up the steps from the bay on to the pier. Notice a small plaque dedicated to 'The Women of Mumbles Head'. A boating disaster in 1883 claimed the lives of the lighthouse keeper's two daughters. Assuming no such problem befalls you, paddle back to the start.

Continue far enough east and you will see Mumbles lighthouse on an offshore island.
(Billy Stock/S)

GETTING THERE

From Swansea, follow the A4067 around Swansea Bay until it reaches the B4433, then follow that road just inland from the sea. As Mumbles Hill rises up to your right (south), pull up in Knab Rock car park, which is adjacent to the slipway from which you will launch. Nearest train station is Swansea. From here, you need to catch two buses to reach The Mumbles – the 4A towards Singleton, then changing at the cricket ground to take the 2A towards Limeslade. Get off at Knab Rock car park.

HIRE & LESSONS

You can hire equipment, or book a lesson or guided tour, from Big Blue Adventures (⌖ explorebigblue.com).

WHERE TO STAY & EAT

Verdi's (⌖ verdis-cafe.co.uk) is a family-run café that overlooks Swansea Bay. Among its offerings is an incredible selection of ice creams that are just what you need after a day of paddling.

19 GOWER POWER

EXPLORE WRECKS & THE 'WURM' AROUND
RHOSSILI BAY, ONE OF THE WORLD'S TOP BEACHES

WHERE	Rhossili Bay, Swansea
STATS	←→ 10km (6¼ miles) round trip ②
START/FINISH	Hillend Burrows, Rhossili Bay ♀ SS415108

Want to visit what is regularly rated one of the world's most beautiful beaches and paddle at the same time? Then head to Rhossili Bay. This remote beach, located on the Gower Peninsula on the south coast of Wales, confronts the Atlantic so, on breezy days, when the force of the oceanic swell kicks in, it is popular with aficionados of watersports (particularly surfers) and aerial sports (paragliders). On windless days, however, the 5km (3 miles) of granular golden sand appeal to those who love a different waterborne activity, namely paddling.

Walkers would argue that the finest views to be gained of this world-beater of a beach come from Gower Way footpath along the cliffs that drop dramatically into the water at either end of the bay. I would disagree. Head out on the water, I say, then look back to enjoy the beach in its bay, its dramatic cliffs leading south to the dragon-like form of the tidal island-cum-headland that Vikings called the 'Wurm', but is now known as Worm's Head. Granted, you have a chance of seeing grey seals and common bottlenose dolphins from the cliff or even the bay, but it is solely from the water that you have the chance of appreciating their inquisitive side and of watching them from their own environment.

PADDLE THIS WAY

The beach at Rhossili is best reached by walking west from the car park at Hillend Burrows. When you reach the shoreline, launch and paddle straight out. Take

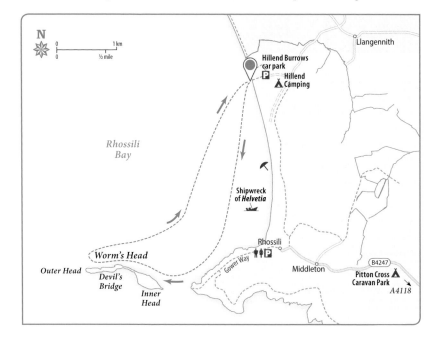

← The remnants of the wreck of the *Helvetia* on the sands of Rhossili Bay, with Worm's Head beyond. (SS)

a moment to look back and around, surveying the land- and waterscapes that surround you. After all, this exposure to the elements is what paddling is all about. Moreover, there's no need for a formal route here – Rhossili is very suitable for following your nose.

Directly below your board, the sea flickers and glistens like diamonds in the sunlight. Cast your eyes back east to the crisply caramel strand before looking up to the brown and grey cliff edges; contrasting and jagged, they frame the setting perfectly. A feast for the eyes indeed. Then… let your other senses unfold until they explode. Taste the salty air; listen to the lapping water or the rush of swell on sand; dip your hands into chilly wateriness. It's hard not to fall in love with Rhossili Bay.

Continue to soak up its dramatic character as you glide south for 2km (1 mile), parallel with the beach, then bear southwest for 1.5km (1 mile). Roughly trace the line of cliffs that lead out towards Worm's Head, the most westerly tip of Gower. Cruise along the north side of Worm's Head, examining its form from the water

↑ Golden sands, cobalt sea: what's not to love about Rhossili Bay? (Ian Woolcock/S)

and decide yourself whether you think its name is worthy. Personally, I find that viewing from the clifftop clearly exposes its shape, but that looking up from the water requires a little more imagination.

There are three parts to Worm's Head. The Inner Head is a flat-topped section that is connected to the mainland by a rocky causeway at low tide. The Inner Head leads west on to a narrow, slightly raised area known as Devil's Bridge (make of that what you will). In turn, this provides access to the Outer Head which, as its name suggests, is the very tip of the 'worm'. Look out for seabirds breeding on the sheer cliffs here, which include guillemot and razorbill.

After you have amply examined Worm's Head, trace its length back east to reach the mainland. Track north along the bay and as you reach the shore, look out for a wooden plinth extending from the sand and leaning back inland. This chunk of wood is what remains of the *Helvetia*, a Norwegian barque that came a cropper in 1887 and is now the Gower's most famous (and most photographed) shipwreck.

Suitably chastened (perhaps…), gently paddle back to the start point. Stay close to the shoreline, people-watching and resolving for yourself why Rhossili Bay never fails to take beachlovers' plaudits.

GETTING THERE

Leave the A4118 at Llanddewi and follow the minor road via Burry Green and Llangennith to Hillend Burrows, where there is a car park (⚲ SS412909). From here, it's an easy walk west on to the beach and launch. Parking further south near Worm's Head involves a steep path down to the beach. Nearest train station is Swansea, from where buses 114, 118 and 119 will get you to the southern access at Rhossili.

HIRE & LESSONS

SUP Gower (⌀ supgower.com) offers equipment hire, lessons and tours.

WHERE TO STAY & EAT

Overlooking Rhossili Bay, The Worm's Head Hotel (⌀ thewormshead.co.uk) operates a bar and restaurant as well as offering accommodation. It also provides paddlers with packed lunches – perfect for beach picnics. There are also two campsites nearby: Pitton Cross Caravan Park (inland of Rhossili; ⌀ pittoncross. co.uk) and Hillend Camping (⌀ hillendcamping.com). The latter is near the Hillend Burrows car park, and also harbours Eddy's café (🕑 Apr–Oct).

TITBITS

At low tide, it is possible to walk across rocks on Worm's Head – something to consider if you have a surfeit of energy. That said, you need to carefully time your walk to avoid getting stranded at high tide, as have many unfortunates before you, poet Dylan Thomas included.

20 WELSH WATERWAY SECRET

PADDLE A CLANDESTINE WATERWAY WITH A LIMESTONE PAST

WHERE	Cresswell River, Pembrokeshire
STATS	←→ 10km (6 miles) return ②
START/FINISH	Cresswell Quay 📍 SN050067

Shhh! Don't tell anyone! Hidden in the Pembrokeshire Coast National Park is what is known as 'Wales's secret waterway'. The rivers that culminate in the Daugeleddau – particularly the Cleddau and Cresswell rivers – collectively take this name. This area makes for a perfect glide through woodland and verdant farmland. The best way of exploring these clandestine channels is by paddling, as this grants easy access to the manifold hidden creeks and sheltered channels. Moreover, the repetitive rhythm of paddling eases the mind and calms the soul – thereby matching your mental state with the tranquillity of your physical surroundings.

Across the union of waterways provided by the Daugeleddau, western and eastern Cleddau, Carew and Cresswell, there are plenty of paddling routes to choose from. The Cleddau in particular provides an abundance of 'A to B' paddles, taking advantage of the tide to ease your journey there and back. One of the most spectacular routes is the gently winding section of the Cresswell River from Cresswell Quay to Lawrenny Quay. This is primarily because of the excitement offered by paddling the dense network of former quarrying creeks.

PADDLE THIS WAY

Begin from Cresswell Quay with its attractive harbour, rows of pastel-toned houses, restored mill, miller's house and traditional pub (Cresselly Arms) tucked

↑ At Lawrenny Quay, life revolves around the water. (David Nicholls)

away behind a low stone wall. Positioned at the tidal limit of the wider Cleddau drainage, the quay is navigable at high tide only – at low tide, you can cross it on stepping stones. So be sure to set off around peak water. As you launch, take a moment to turn round and admire the village from the water.

Head downstream for 2km (1¼ miles) as the river meanders through rolling countryside. You will pass sprays of woodland stippled with limestone houses. Just after you spy the village of West Williamston, set back along a channel to your left (south), look along the same shore to see a series of seven manmade channels that have been cut into the bank. These incisions were made during the 18th century, when limestone was quarried from the river shores (including to make the houses you spotted upstream).

You could easily spend several happy hours dipping in and out of these narrow cuts. Some of the longer channels – being overgrown, with moss-covered rocks and tree roots bulging over the banks – can make you feel like you are discovering a lost world. This is precisely the sort of adventure to which paddling is ideally suited. Don't rush this section. Indulge your inner Indiana.

Following the abandonment of quarrying, nature has been taking over the wider area. Saltmarsh has spread to provide welcome habitat for waders such as redshank and curlew, plus cormorant and even small mammals such as short-tailed field vole. Moreover, the nearby Wildlife Trust reserve at West Williamston is renowned among conservationists as holding a key population of a rare butterfly, the brown hairstreak. It flies in August and September – but don't expect to see it from the water!

At this point, the Carew River joins from your left (south). Ignore this and continue downstream. The hours can vanish along this stretch of water, so it pays to remain mindful of tides (remember what happens at Cresswell Quay at low tide…). To your left (south) the shore is fringed with woodland that disguises

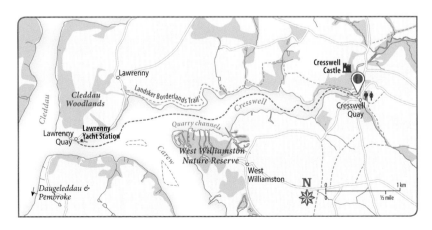

↑ Canoeing along the Cresswell, flanked by verdant woodland. (Pete Ward/The Real Adventure Company)

a hinterland of arable fields. Ahead of you, the channel may start to become lined with moored yachts. To your right (north), after 1.5km (1 mile), the sleepy village of Lawrenny Quay will start to materialise. This marks the start of the Cleddau proper, as the Cresswell pours into it and the swollen river continues south towards the sea.

Finish the outward part of your paddle at one of two pontoons either side of Lawrenny Yacht Station. Walking ashore, you could explore the National Trust property of Cleddau (with its steep-sided, ancient, oak-rich woodlands) or seek refreshment in the local pub (The Lawrenny Arms) or, better still, Quayside, a charming café offering uninterrupted views over the waterway and a daily menu offering fresh, local seafood.

Once reinvigorated, simply paddle back east upriver to Cresswell Quay. If you still have energy when you arrive at the village, and should the tide remain conveniently high, you could extend the paddle northwards by 500m (⅓ mile) to admire the ruins of Cresswell Castle. Carved from stone in the 13th century, the vestiges of the fort are located at the highest navigable point of the river.

GETTING THERE

Leave the A40 on the A4075, heading south towards Pembroke. At Cresselly, turn west along a minor road to Cresswell Quay. There is parking along the roadside near the public toilet at the north end of the village. You can launch from here too.

HIRE & LESSONS

The Real Adventure Company (⊘ therealadventurecompany.com) provides guided tours along the upper reaches of the Cleddau. If you want to explore further afield, however, you'll need your own equipment.

WHERE TO STAY & EAT

Lawrenny Quay village (⊘ lawrennyyachtstation.co.uk) has a community-run hostel (⊘ lawrennyhostel. com), which returns its profits to the community. The environs of Lawrenny Quay have several B&Bs and farmstays (eg: ⊘ tinyurl.com/farmstay-pembroke), self-catering cottages and campsites. For food, try the Lawrenny Arms (✆ 01646 651439) or Quayside (⊘ quaysidelawrenny.co.uk) in Lawrenny Quay, or Cresselly Arms in Cresswell Quay (✆ 01646 651210).

TITBITS

For the intermediate-level paddlers, it is possible to continue from Lawrenny Quay downstream along the Cleddau and Daugleddau ('two Cleddaus') until you reach the town of Pembroke. However, this trip is nothing short of a marathon. It should neither be done alone nor without a companion who has experience and knowledge of these waters.

21 LOCKS, BANBURY CAKES & DREAMING SPIRES

INDULGE YOURSELF WITH TWO-PLUS DAYS EXPLORING THE HEART OF ENGLAND ALONG THE OXFORD CANAL

WHERE	Oxford Canal, Oxfordshire
STATS	←→ 62km (39 miles) ⌛ Best tackled over 2–3 days Locks: 31 ⓘ
START	Fenny Marina ⦿ SP428528
FINISH	Hythe Bridge, Oxford ⦿ SP508063

he wonderful thing about canals is that they are largely unaffected by tides and winds so planning adventures doesn't leave you at the mercy of the elements. However, there is one considerable downside. Locks. If you're paddling for a single day or even a couple of days, most people will find it bearable to traverse these chambers with gates at either end. For any long-distance touring expedition, however, portaging (carrying a boat between two waters) becomes an arduous task because of the cumbersome kit you're lugging around. When gauging the likely length of your days, it's worth allocating up to 10 minutes per lock to transport your board/canoe/kayak.

The Oxford Canal runs for 126km (78 miles) through central England. It links the Coventry Canal in the north to the River Thames in the south, and also is integrated with the Grand Union Canal between Royal Leamington Spa and Daventry. The Oxford Canal's southern section, between Oxford city centre and Napton-on-the-Hill, is largely unspoilt yet also gives a glimpse of how life around the canals would have been two centuries ago during the heyday of waterborne trade.

For all its historical charm, however, Napton is most notable (to the point of notoriety) among boaters for its extensive series of locks in all-too-quick succession The flight is coined locally as 'Heartbreak Hill', a fitting name for a section of the waterways that had me in tears of exhaustion as I paddled the length of England. You'll be pleased to hear this route avoids this particularly galling section.

As you paddle the canal, notice the old lift-bridges that are sprinkled along its length. Traditionally, these were used by farmers to move livestock across the canal and into nearby fields. Most are no longer operational; their only modern purpose seems to be to lend texture and charm to an already picturesque waterway. The good news is that you won't have to portage these bridges as they are mostly high enough for canoeists and kayakers to paddle underneath. Paddlers aboard SUPs can travel through provided they sit or kneel.

PADDLE THIS WAY

This is a hefty paddle, best enjoyed over two–three days. This means breaking the journey with overnight stops (for suggestions, see *Where to stay & eat*, page 113).

Launch from Fenny Marina, then paddle south towards Oxford (though no problems if you prefer to start at the latter city and head north). The first 2km (1¼ miles) meanders along a mainly narrow canal lined with tall trees that rather prevent you from enjoying too much of the surrounding landscape. After a further 1km (⅔ mile) you'll pass a reservoir on the left (east) that heralds the first of a five-lock series that you will have to portage – so get ready. You then have a choice, partly dependent on the amount of equipment you are carrying. Either portage all five locks in a single, relatively long walk – around 700m (½ mile) – or dip the board in and out of the water at each lock.

← Narrowboats are a regular feature along the Oxford Canal, particularly at the university city itself. (SS)

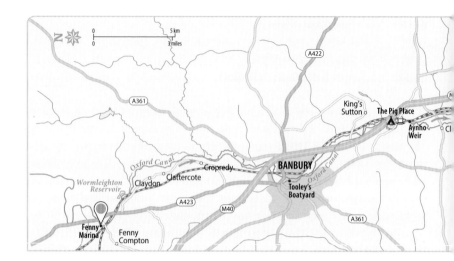

Beyond the locks the trees become more scattered, enabling the views to evolve into sweeping landscapes of farmland and pasture grazed by cattle. A couple of waterside farmhouses are the only clues that you are then passing the charming Oxfordshire villages of Claydon and Clattercote, which are both set back from the water and thus unnoticed by paddlers.

After a further three locks, at around 6km (3¾ miles) from the start, you get your first sniff of civilisation. The village of Cropredy is characterised by thatched stone cottages, Gothic ironstone church and two traditional pubs, which are perfect for 'refuelling' (see *Where to stay & eat*, page 113).

Back on the water, the next 5km (3 miles) winds round three wide bends and through flat, open countryside. The towpath is popular with dog walkers, who are often keen to chat as you paddle along at walking pace. In this stretch you are likely to see mallards and moorhens, and with the protection of water voles on the Oxford Canal in recent years, you might strike lucky with one of these enchanting yet endangered mammals.

A swift 6.5km (4 miles) south, passing through fields stretching almost as far as the eye can see and burrowing underneath the M40, you arrive in the beating heart of Banbury. The town is famous for its eponymous 'Cross' (think of the nursery rhyme line: 'Ride a cock horse to Banbury Cross') and cakes. The latter, a local speciality, are flat pastries filled with spicy currants that have followed a secret recipe since at least the 1580s; plenty of Banbury bakeries sell them, so it's easy to indulge. Perhaps more of an acquired taste, but certainly more important, Banbury is also home to the famous Tooley's Boatyard that sits alongside the canal as you pass through the town. It is the oldest dry dock in England's inland waterways, operating continuously since 1790.

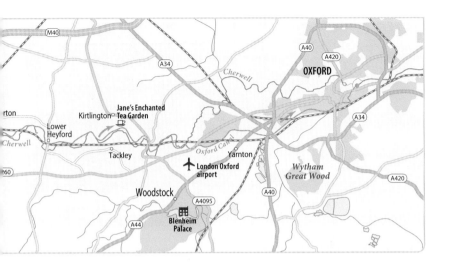

↑ Taking a well-earned breather on the Oxford Canal; it's a long route! (Neil Irwin)

Leaving Banbury southwards, you'll notice that the faster-flowing River Cherwell runs just metres from the Oxford Canal; in places the two waterways share the same towpath. After 10km (6¼ miles) – and 11 locks! – you'll reach The Pig Place: look out for the armchairs and fire pits dotted along a small hill on the towpath. This rather kooky place is more than just a pitstop. It's also a campsite should you be ready to get some rest after a long day paddling. A decent option to ready yourself to continue into Oxfordshire the following day.

About 4km (2½ miles) after Banbury, you reach Aynho Weir. At the lock the River Cherwell effectively crosses the canal diagonally. Admire the brickwork arches that carry the canal's towpath across the river. (Note: heavy rainfall can make currents strong here and hard to paddle against.)

Passing Lower Heyford, you paddle parallel with a railway line (to your left) and London Oxford airport (to your right) as you make the final descent through rural Oxfordshire into the city of dreaming spires – Oxford. While the route is mostly open fields, there is one sparkling jewel to look out for around 6km (3¾ miles) south of Lower Heyford. As you pass Kirtlington, Jane's Enchanted Tea Garden is nestled quietly away on the left/west bank. With its quirky furniture and flamboyant style, there is much to tempt you in for a quick coffee and cake. And I can thoroughly recommend the rhubarb crumble!

Replenished, return to the water. Savour the final section of greenness – meadows, fields and allotments – before reaching Oxford's built-up outskirts. Anticipation grows as you approach the real gem of this city. Look straight ahead to spot the pale ivory 'dreaming spires' of the University of Oxford, a term coined by Matthew Arnold in his poem 'Thyrsis' published in 1865.

If you are paddling alongside the Varsity town's parks and meadows in summer, you will probably notice hordes of other people punting and boating – all of you enjoying the waterways. What a glorious culmination to this paddling

↑ Within the confines of the city, the Oxford Canal can get a little crowded in summer. (SS)

adventure – to be on the water amid the architecturally breathtaking colleges that make up the oldest university in the English-speaking world.

In the city centre, the end of the Oxford Canal is clearly marked by, well, the end of the canal. Egress here on to the towpath. Were you to head right (west), you would be taking a cut through to the River Thames. Although fun, this is an altogether different level of adventure. Instead, explore Oxford.

GETTING THERE

Fenny Marina (thefennymarina.co.uk) is on the Oxford Canal between bridges 136 and 137; turn west off the A423 towards Fenny Compton. Car parking is adjacent to the marina, from where you can easily access the water. I suggest travelling as a team and leaving a car at either end of the route. If that doesn't work for you, your best bet is to take a taxi back to Fenny Marina. As is often the case with rural routes, public transport is not really practicable here.

HIRE & LESSONS

Get More Adventure (getmoreadventure.com) provides kit, equipment, tours and lessons.

WHEN TO GO

The Oxford Canal teems with boaters during summer holidays, so head out late spring through to the end of June for a much quieter experience.

WHERE TO STAY & EAT

In Cropredy, The Brasenose Arms (brasenosearms.com) is a traditional inn serving delicious, hearty food and also offering accommodation. Being set back from the water, it is a short walk to get there but the large beer garden means there is plenty of space to leave your equipment. Even closer to the canal is The Red Lion (01295 758680), where log fires warm up any paddler braving this route in winter. Just outside Banbury, canalside camping (adults only) is available at The Pig Place (thepigplace.co.uk; Mar–Oct), which also serves delicious cooked breakfasts featuring local produce. If you don't stay here, you're best off wild camping (page 11). British Waterways is happy for people to camp alongside towpaths and at rural locks, as long as access is not blocked. Near Kirtlington, Jane's Enchanted Tea Garden (janes-cream-teas.moonfruit.com; reopens 2019) is a cracking independent café serving delicious homemade sweet treats. Book ahead for its 'Full Jeeves' high tea!

TITBITS

One downside to this paddle is the quantity of plastic waste nestled among the reeds – an unfortunate legacy of population growth in towns such as Banbury. As responsible paddlers I urge you to do your bit and try to remove a few pieces as you paddle. Don't forget to log what you find in the Plastic Patrol smartphone app (page 16).

22 THE ONLY WAY IS ESSEX

NAVIGATE PAST PREJUDICE & STEREOTYPE TO EXPERIENCE THE REAL ESSEX — CHARMING, TRANQUIL & QUINTESSENTIALLY ENGLISH

WHERE	Chelmer and Blackwell Navigation, Essex
STATS	←→ 8km (5 miles) return ①
START/FINISH	Paper Mill Lock, Little Baddow ⚲ TL777090

Mention the word 'Essex' and a succession of rather brash or boring stereotypes may spring to mind. Put any such thoughts to one side, and instead let yourself be surprised by the county through a visit to the River Chelmer and its waterway subsidiary, the Chelmer and Blackwater Navigation. Even if you're already an Essex fan, this paddle will enable to you to experience an altogether different side of this county.

The River Chelmer belongs entirely to the county of Essex. It begins in Debden near Thaxted, flowing 65km (40 miles) from near the county's northwest border, through Chelmsford, before joining forces with the River Blackwater and flowing into the North Sea near Maldon. The Chelmer and Blackwater Navigation comprises 22km (14 miles) of canal that connects the two rivers; this route sits roughly in the middle.

Originally, the Chelmer was named the River Baddow, which may be derived from the Old English for 'bad water' or for 'birch stream'. Today, the Chelmer is a river with pristine waters and picturesque views, both reason enough for its inclusion in this book. While this waterway still divulges clues to its industrial past from beneath its low-hanging willows, the section featuring this route – between Little Baddow and Ulting, midway between Chelmsford and Maldon – harbours fine, unspoilt and quintessentially English countryside plus a notably beautiful stone church.

PADDLE THIS WAY

Launch from the banks of the quaint Paper Mill Lock north of Little Baddow and head east, downstream, in the direction of Ulting. The waters are lined with

↑ A group kayaking along the Chelmer. (Essex Waterways)

canal boats as you head east towards Ulting. Beyond the banks, when you can see through rows of trees, are open fields. The adjacent towpath is less busy than you might imagine, seemingly only being frequented by dog walkers, cyclists and joggers 'in the know'.

Continue heading east on the Chelmer towards the Blackwater Navigation, largely passing through arable countryside. Although the expansive fields are a little samey, cookie-cutter views coupled with the serenity of the Chelmer are certainly nothing to complain about. Nearby villages are set well back from the river too, and thus invisible to the paddler. The exception is Ulting, and what an anomaly it is.

This village has history, having hosted England's first sugar-beet factory, which served it well until the industry was undercut by cheaper imports of sugarcane. Fortunately, such a reduction in economic significance appears to have had a negligible impact on the village's unbridled beauty. Pride of place goes to Ulting's charming stone church, which has stood on Chelmer's north bank since the mid 12th century and retains magnificent features dating back to the 13th century. Paddlers may pull up to the bank – which was coloured by daffodils when I visited in spring – and cross its atmospheric graveyard to reach the church entrance. If the door is open, take a respectful peek inside and soak up its old-style charm.

Another 1km (⅔ mile) downstream is Hoe Mill Lock. This is a quiet section of the waterway, rarely used by the motorboats you'll find towards Maldon. Even better, trees shelter the river pool: a lovely spot for paddling, indeed. Stay back from Hoe Mill Lock itself, however, as this is a sensitive fishing area.

Retrace your route to Paper Mill Lock and haul out. If you have been inspired to see more of Essex, walk into Little Baddow. As well as a church (Saint Mary the Virgin) with a 14th-century door (known as 'Devil's Door') that sits 1.5km (1 mile) west of the village, Little Baddow has two pubs, on the off chance that you're ready for some refreshment.

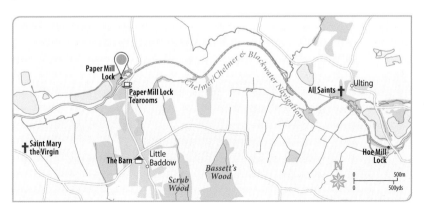

GETTING THERE

From the A12 at junction 19, take the B1137 towards Hatfield Peverel. About 1km after Boreham, turn right (southeast) to follow minor roads towards Little Baddow. Stop at Paper Mill Lock, where there is roadside parking and a small car park next to the Paper Mill Lock Tea Rooms. Launch from the lock. Nearest train station is Hatfield Peverel and the nearest bus stop is Boreham. From either town it is a bit of a hike; private transport is more practical here.

HIRE & LESSONS

The nearest paddleboarding provider is SUPsect ( supsect.com), which has a base in Chelmsford and uses the River Chelmer.

WHERE TO STAY & EAT

Paper Mill Lock Tea Rooms (🖉 papermilllock.co.uk; 🕐 closed Mon–Tue in Dec–Jan) is an ideal spot for light lunch or a good old cream tea. Dogs permitted. The Barn B&B (🖉 pilgrimsbarn.co.uk) is a converted Grade-2-listed building in Little Baddow.

TITBITS

For a guide to the Chelmer and Blackwater Navigation, see 🖉 waterways.org.uk/pdf/essex_flyer. You need a special licence from the Inland Waterways Association to paddle the Chelmer and Blackwater Navigation (🖉 tinyurl.com/chelmer-licence). The 24-hour option is cheap.

Sedge-fringed and tree-lined, the Chelmer Canal is a bucolic waterway. (Tom Curtis/S)

23 JEWEL IN THE CROWN

START AT AN ENORMOUS GEM OF A BEACH THEN EXPLORE HIDDEN CAVES & TOWERING CLIFFS

WHERE	Newgale, Pembrokeshire
STATS	←→ 14km (8⅔ miles) return ③
START/FINISH	Newgale beach 📍 SM846223

With sea to its south, west and northwest, Pembrokeshire has become a no-brainer destination for SUP, canoe and kayak activity. There is simply so much choice! The county's coastline is filled with Blue Flag beaches and hidden coastal gems. Amid this treasure hoard, Newgale is surely the crowning jewel. Also a recipient of the Blue Flag, Newgale offers a spacious strand with expansive flat sand backed by a pebble beach that 'arrived' after a storm in 1859.

Moreover, Newgale has long been Wales's most special place for watersports. Offering much more than simply open water, it is a beach like no other. Here you are spoilt for choice. You could paddle 3km (2 miles) of uninterrupted clear water. Or you could head towards the cliff lines that run along each side of the beach to discover fascinating rock formations, veiled caves, curious seals and a secluded cove that is simply perfect for a bit of respite.

The well-trodden Pembrokeshire Coast Path runs along the beach before treading up the nearby cliffs, offering views over the water, its seabirds and its seals. However, as is the beauty of paddling, from the water you'll be right in the thick of the action – the best seat in the show.

PADDLE THIS WAY

Newgale beach is a great spot for a leisurely paddle, following the sand edge wherever the whim takes you. However, if you want more of an adventure, you

↑ Boats dot the river southwards from Solva towards the rocky Pembrokeshire coast. (Billy Stock/S)

can follow the cliff line – firstly northwest, then west – until you reach the River Solva, which you can follow north to the village of the same name.

At mid- to low tide set off from Newgale beach itself, and head northwest, following the cliff edge. Keep your eyes peeled. Atlantic grey seals often frequent the nooks and crannies here. The mammals' curious nature means you're likely to get a very personal experience if you're nearby.

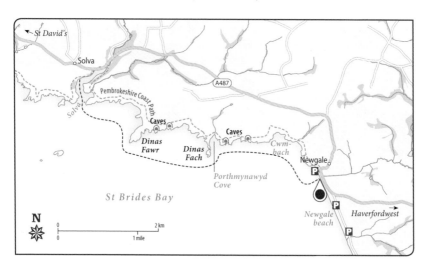

↑ This paddle rewards the curious: investigate caves and other rocky nooks and crannies. (Peter Guess/S)

Carpeted with green, towering sea cliffs undulate along the sides of the beach. Down below, caves provide great adventure for the inquisitive paddler. Enter them carefully to admire the shapes and textures of the rocks – all a result of interaction with the water. If the tide is out you'll get the chance to rest at secluded beaches along the way. A favourite of mine is Porthmynawyd Cove (pronounced 'Porth-min-ar-wid), which sits about 500m (⅓ mile) from the north end of Newgale beach, just before you reach the headland called Dinas Fach. There's something magical about sinking your feet into the sands of an empty bay, without a single other soul or footprint in sight. And the beauty of a coastal location is that the tide will soon wash away evidence of your visit too.

About 1km (⅔ mile) beyond a headland called Dinas Fawr, the coast cedes to a wide opening that marks the mouth of the River Solva. Paddle right (north) into the steep-sided valley, taking care to mind any boats lining the river edge. A few kayak and canoe clubs are based in Solva village, so watch out for fellow watersport enthusiasts!

As you approach the attractive harbour village, you'll see a little café on your left, called Café on the Quay. Pull ashore on the banks outside and take advantage of their homemade cakes. If you have the time, make sure to explore Solva; just take the Pembrokeshire Coast Path that runs behind the café and follow it northeast into the village. Once you are done, paddle back east to your starting point at Newgale beach, keeping mindful of the tides. To facilitate your passage, you would ideally be returning on the flow of a high tide but provided winds are minimal this is not essential.

GETTING THERE

Newgale lies on the A487 between Haverfordwest and St David's. There are three car parks just south of the village, alongside Newgale beach. Park up and launch. The nearest train station is Haverfordwest, from where it would be best to take a taxi for the remaining 10km (6¼ miles) to Newgale.

HIRE & LESSONS

Big Blue Adventures (⌀ explorebigblue.com) can provide equipment hire, lessons or guided tours around Newgale and other locations on the Welsh coast.

WHERE TO STAY & EAT

In Solva, stop for homemade delights at Café on the Quay (✆ 01437 721725). Sands Café (✆ 01437 729222) is tucked away just behind Newgale beach. The beachfront location of Newgale Camping Site (⌀ newgalecampingsite.co.uk) renders it the perfect spot for a relaxed weekend getaway. Solva has various options for B&Bs, including Pen y Banc (⌀ penybanc.co.uk).

24 THE DEEP

BRAVE DEEP WATERS JUST OFFSHORE FROM A PEMBROKESHIRE PORT WITH QUITE SOME HISTORY

WHERE	Fishguard, Pembrokeshire
STATS	↔ 6km (3¾ miles) return ③ – ④
START/FINISH	Lower Town Quay slipway ♀ SM960903

Tucked snugly at the feet of Fishguard, where the River (Afon) Gwaun reaches St George's Channel is a lovely little coastal village known locally as Lower Town. Pretty pastel-coloured, grey and white houses string along the quay. In its heyday of the 18th century Lower Town was a nationally important trading and fishing harbour. Today it is Fishguard that is better known, being a major port for ferries between Wales and Ireland.

Fishguard has history itself, however, being famous for the last failed invasion of Britain in 1797. Legend has it that French troops arriving at Fishguard mistook hundreds of scarlet-clad women – Fishguard residents dressed in traditional scarlet tunics – for British Army redcoats and turned their boats around. The fascinating story is told in an embroidered tapestry that is housed in the library at Fishguard town hall.

↑ Only experienced paddlers should test themselves in the deep waters and rocky shores of Fishguard Bay. (Higstone/S)

As you prepare to paddle from Lower Town quay into open water you can feel the drama of the landscape. Steep, rocky slopes texture the otherwise delicate fishing village. Down at sea level, paddling enables you to closely examine the fascinating rock formations – and even the limpets that grow on them! Quays generally need deep water, which means that you may not need to travel too far to spot Atlantic grey seal, harbour porpoise or common bottlenose dolphin. Such quick access to deep water (and to craggy caves) also means that this route is recommended only for experienced paddlers, or for those with a guide.

PADDLE THIS WAY

Launch at high tide and follow the route as you are gently propelled by the current. To your back, a panorama of green hills contrasts with the deep blue of the water. If you launch from the quay's outermost point, you'll have already passed the small sailing boats moored up, but if you start further back you'll need to jink through them. Follow the towering cliff edge to your left (west) or right (east) and you'll experience fabulous rock formations featuring hidden bays and caves.

As you paddle north, look left (west) to see if you can spot the Battle of Fishguard cannons. To your right, the stone wall of the inner quay comes to an end just northwest of the Fishguard Bay Yacht Club. North of here is another fort, sat atop a promontory called Castle Point.

Novice paddlers should stay within the harbour, which provides ample shelter. More experienced paddlers, however, may continue roughly northeast along the rugged coastline for 5km (3¼ miles) past some seriously impressive rock formations. In particular, look out for Needle Rock around 3.5km (2 miles) along.

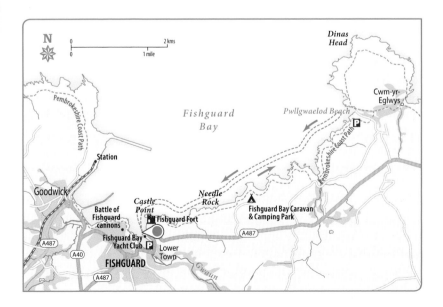

It stands at more than 50m tall and has an opening (an 'eye'), through which you can paddle. Bet you never thought you'd fit through the eye of a needle…

Fishguard Bay Caravan and Camping Park is 500m (⅓ mile) beyond Needle Rock. It marks the final stretch to the small sandy cove of Pwllgwaelod Beach. The coastline here doesn't really allow you to be non-committal at high tide. It largely comprises towering cliffs and rocky outcrops with only a sprinkling of coves. Although beautiful, this can make for an intimidating journey for the less experienced paddler who may not quite know their limits; ocean paddling can bring on fatigue more quickly than on still waters inland.

Comprising dark sand and shingle, Pwllgwaelod Beach attracts both locals and tourists looking for a peaceful spot to while away the day. Dramatic cliffs surround the beach and, either side of the cove, rocks lurk malevolently just below the surface – a combination that renders Pwllgwaelod unsuitable for watersports such as surfing, but popular at low tide for some rockpooling action.

Once you are moored, take in the spectacular views west across Fishguard Bay. Being secluded, this is a prime spot for picnicking paddlers. That said, there

↑ Paddling beneath the steep, rocky cliffs of Fishguard Bay (Pete Ward/The Real Adventure Company)

is also a small pub set just back from the beach (and at the start of a delightful wooded valley) that may warrant your attention. The Old Sailors dates back to 1593 and retains some original features. The pub's original name, Sailor's Safety, is a reference to the light beamed out continuously to help guide fishermen back to shore (and, indeed, this remains a landing spot for those harvesting the sea's bounty, including lobsters caught at Dinas Head, or Ynys Dinas, just to the north). If the tide permits and the sky is clear of cloud, hang around for a while. Facing west, this spot is justly renowned for its magnificent summer sunsets.

Talking of Dinas Head… the waters beyond Pwllgwaelod curve round some of Pembrokeshire's most rugged and picturesque coast, culminating in that north-facing headland. Make no mistake, these waters can be perilous and are best not paddled. Instead, consider dispensing with your board for a while to explore overland – hiking the well-marked footpath (Pembrokeshire Coast Path) that tracks the circumference of the promontory for 5km (3 miles). Once you've had your fill retrace your route.

GETTING THERE

Fishguard lies at the junction of the A40 (from Haverfordwest) and A487 (from Cardigan). The latter runs along the quay at Lower Town, with car parking by the bridge over the River (Afon) Gwaun (SM962371). Launch from the nearby concrete slipway. Nearest train station is Fishguard Harbour, from where you can catch bus 410 to The Square in Lower Town, which is a short walk from the launch point at the quay.

HIRE & LESSONS

Big Blue Adventures (explorebigblue.com) have kit and equipment available and as the route is quite demanding they can even take you out on guided tours if you are concerned about completing this without guidance. Based at Lower Town, Board Games Surfing (boardgamessurfing.com) provides SUP hire and lessons. The Real Adventure Company (therealadventurecompany.com) provides guided tours here and elsewhere in Pembrokeshire.

WHERE TO STAY & EAT

At Pwllgwaelod Beach, be sure to visit The Old Sailors pub (theoldsailors.co.uk). There are a few pubs and eateries in Fishguard including The Ship Inn. Details plus information on overnight accommodation are assembled at gofishguard.co.uk.

TITBITS

This route, like all coastal routes, is not a light undertaking. You must be aware of conditions and tides before setting out. Even for experienced paddlers in fine weather, the return trip to Pwllgwaelod Beach will take a full day.

25 VARSITY VA-VA-VOOM

FAVOUR PADDLEBOARDING OVER PUNTING IN THE UNIVERSITY TOWN OF CAMBRIDGE

WHERE	River Cam, Cambridgeshire
STATS	←→ 10km (6¼ miles) return ①
START/FINISH	Jesus Lock, Cambridge 📍 TL450592

The River Cam flows through Cambridge, eventually feeding the River Great Ouse. As well as its university, Cambridge is famous for its punting. Nevertheless, there's plenty of space for paddling of a different kind. So why not mix things up a bit? And if you like to be rewarded with inspiring architecture and history on your travels, this journey is one for you.

This gentle adventure takes you south past the dramatic Cambridge colleges, where you'll weave between the many punters. Rather than resent the incursion on your motion, relish the hustle and bustle for its opportunities to watch people and admire architecture (particularly the marvellous Bridge of Sighs) before getting back to business.

If you need a rest, stop at each bridge to see what's on offer. Otherwise, keep paddling and you'll eventually meet Mill Pond and its weir, where the grassy area of Coe Fen may throng with summer picnickers. Follow the river upstream and you'll hit the village of Grantchester, which is home to a delightful little tea garden called The Orchard Tea Garden. Many a luminary has sipped tea or nibbled a fresh scone here – from Virginia Woolf and Rupert Brooke to HRH Prince Charles. Do the same while soaking up the atmosphere and pondering the age-old question: what comes first on the scone – cream or jam?

↑ The imposing King's College Chapel on the banks of the River Cam. (Pajor Pawel/S)

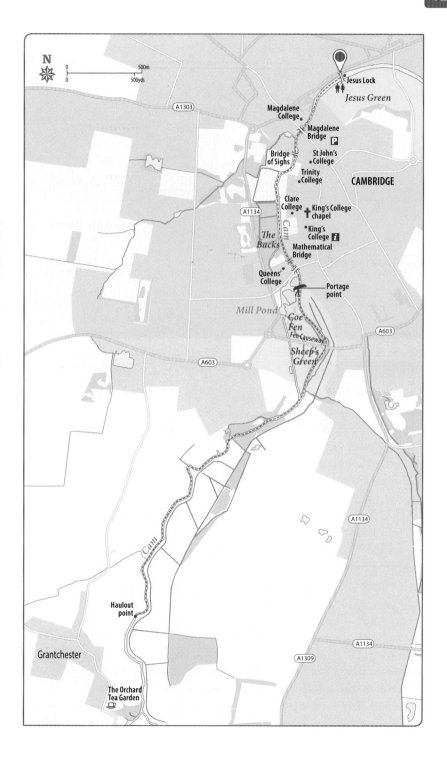

PADDLE THIS WAY

Launch from the River Cam at Jesus Lock (located on Jesus Green) and head west – upstream – past a peppering of buildings, moored narrow boats and punts, mixed with parkland and weeping willows that hang pendulously over the water. There are many signs that you are not in deep countryside: people walking along the towpath or punting on the Cam, private gardens backing on to the water, and the A1134 road that hems The Backs, parallel with the Cam. Yet none of this comparative hubris prevents the scene from being calm and peaceful.

This route passes some of Britain's most historic architecture. This starts with the first bridge you pass. Magdalene Bridge takes its name from the college positioned just behind it. Notice the rows of punts for rent – unless it's the height of summer, in which case they will be all in use, so you'll be dodging them instead.

Continue paddling beneath ever more abundant weeping willows while marvelling at further stunning buildings as they cleave into view. As you start the approach to Trinity College, you will see another bridge – one more striking and famous than any other you will have encountered on your previous paddles.

Located at St John's College, the Bridge of Sighs is named after a bridge in Venice. Although both are covered, they are otherwise architecturally very different. Tourists love this neo-Gothic, Grade-1-listed number, and it's not hard to see why. It's a wonder, especially as you look up from the water, and worth a visit to the Cam in its own right.

↑ The Bridge of Sighs – a little piece of Venice in Cambridge. (Ilia Torlin/S)

Continue south towards King's College and its 15th-century chapel – an architectural delight featuring intricate medieval stained glass – then traverse Clare and Queens' colleges to reach the next bridge. Although not quite the architectural delight of the Bridge of Sighs, this one is no less fascinating. Indeed, the aptly named Mathematical Bridge is a true brain-boggler. It is a wooden structure that takes the shape of an arch. This leads one to assume that it is made from curved material. Wrong. It is actually made using entirely straight timbers. Unusual engineering at its most sophisticated!

As you paddle south towards Mill Pond, you will need to portage. When you can't go any further, simply swing right into a small side channel which curves back towards the main river and, when this ends, portage over the footpath and back into the main channel among the moored-up punts.

Beyond Coe Fen, Sheep's Green and Fen Causeway, the city fades and the landscape transforms into grazing pasture and cultivation. Even more willows – my absolute favourite tree, if you hadn't already guessed – line the banks, creating a sensation of enchantment on this increasingly bucolic, rural waterway.

A further 3km (1¾ miles) from the Mathematical Bridge and you'll reach the village of Grantchester. To your right (west), a small bank will likely be full of punts. Pull up here then head along the narrow marked path to take scones and tea at The Orchard Tea Garden. Then return to the water and retrace your route.

GETTING THERE

From the M11 junction 13, take the A1303 east into Cambridge. Parking is tricky in town; the nearest car park is on Park Street (⊘ cambridge.gov.uk/park-street-car-park). From here, walk north to Park Parade then across Jesus Green to the launch point at Jesus Lock. Alternatively, leave your car at the park & ride immediately east of junction 13 of the M11. Nearest train station is Cambridge, from where you can catch the Citi 3 bus to Christ's College then walk 800m (½ mile) to Jesus Lock.

HIRE & LESSONS

Although there are punts available to hire along the River Cam, you'll need to bring your own paddleboard for this adventure.

WHERE TO STAY & EAT

As you pass through Cambridge there are a few restaurants along the Cam just before you reach Magdalene Bridge; this route is also ideal for a riverside picnic. You will have to paddle a little further south to get there (and then stroll west into the village), but The Orchard Tea Garden in Grantchester (⊘ theorchardteagarden. co.uk) is a delightful spot for a break. Indeed, it would be an offence not to take advantage of its large, deckchair-filled gardens, especially on a warm summer's day.

26 AS YOU LIKE IT

PADDLE THE STRATFORD CANAL THROUGH THE FORMER FOREST OF ARDEN, LOVED BY SHAKESPEARE

WHERE	Stratford Canal, West Midlands
STATS	↔ 19.2km (12 miles) return ①
START/FINISH	Drawbridge Road, Major's Green 📍 SP103780

Y ou might not expect there to be a tranquil, rural waterway in the heavily urbanised West Midlands. But the 42km (25½ miles) of the Stratford Canal, which lies in two sections in the south of the region, is precisely that. Expect a gentle paddle that will carry you peacefully through rolling grassland, past little villages and under original redbrick bridges.

Even better for those paddlers for whom the word 'canal' evokes an unpleasant experience lugging your board overland, there's not a single lock to portage on the route from Major's Green south to Hockley Heath. That said, were you to carry on further, you would swiftly get your comeuppance. Lapworth Flight is a series of 18 locks in quick succession: not a light undertaking. One for the energetic among you!

PADDLE THIS WAY

Start from lock 8 (sometimes known as Shirley Drawbridge) on the Stratford Canal, on Drawbridge Road in Major's Green, south of Solihull. Take advantage

↑ Overhanging willows are a striking characteristic of the banks of the Stratford Canal. (SS)

of easy access from the banks and paddle south. Once you have passed under Haslucks Green Road and a railway bridge, you'll be immersed in heavily vegetated countryside. Here tall reedbeds escape the water's surface and overgrown shrubs narrow the canal. On the east bank (next to the towpath), a number of boats moor up – some with pretty 'gardens' and potted plants on their roofs.

The landscape opens up into grassy fields. See if you can spot a hefty veteran oak tree standing in sorry solitude on the left (east) bank. It was once part of the Forest of Arden which, in its medieval heyday, extended from Stratford-upon-Avon in Warwickshire to Tamworth in Staffordshire. Encompassing great tracts of land that are now under the concrete of cities such as Coventry and Birmingham, the forest was known to local lad William Shakespeare, who mentioned it in his play *As You Like It*.

After around 1.5km (1 mile), you pass along the fringes of a new village, Dickens Heath. This results in a swell of people (particularly walking dogs) along the towpath. By now you may have spotted that bridges over the canal are all clearly

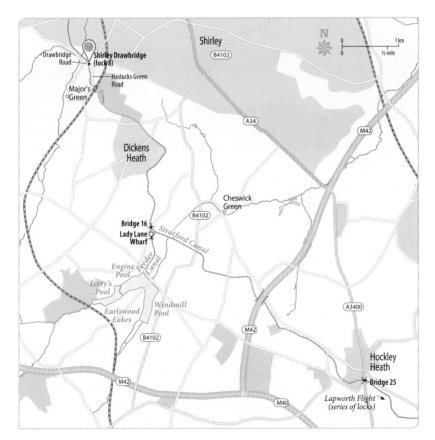

numbered with obvious plates. Take your bearings from these. If you're peckish when you reach the boat mooring at bridge 16, pull up as Lady Lane Wharf is a bar that serves food.

Look out for the small slipway on the left (east) just beyond this bridge. Here a feeder canal leads to Earlswood Lakes, three manmade reservoirs (Windmill Pool, Terry's Pool and Engine Pool) built in the 1820s. If you have time these reservoirs can be paddled. You may even spot a couple of sailing boats from the local club.

Continue about 3km (1¾ miles), traversing grassy fields and limbering under three bridges until you pass beneath the M42 flyover. Then it's about the same distance again, this time parallel with a minor road that connects a couple of farms until you enter the village of Hockley Heath and reach bridge 25 (which is where the A3400 runs over the canal). This is as far as you will go on this paddle – unless you fancy confronting the Lapworth Flight. Either paddle back to base or exit here and rehydrate at The Wharf Tavern, a small pub right by bridge 25 in Hockley Heath.

↑ Detour off the Stratford Canal to explore Earlswood Lakes. (Peter Cox/A)

GETTING THERE

Leave the A435 at Wythall and take the minor road via Tidbury Green to reach Major's Green. Turn off Haslucks Green Road on to Drawbridge Road and park on the roadside opposite The Drawbridge Inn. Nearest train station is Shirley, which connects to mainline service at Birmingham Moor Street. From Shirley station, take Haslucks Green Road south for 600m (⅓ mile) to the launch point.

HIRE & LESSONS

Limited hire options locally, so having your own equipment is helpful.

WHERE TO STAY & EAT

Just beyond bridge 16, the Lady Lane Wharf (ladylanewharf.co.uk) is a bar serving food. There is a no-frills menu at The Wharf Tavern (tinyurl.com/thewharftavern) located beside the Stratford Canal at the end of the paddle route.

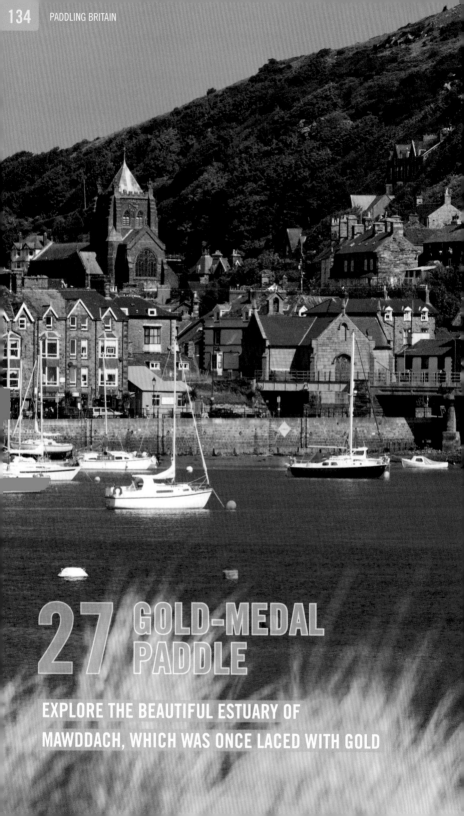

27 GOLD-MEDAL PADDLE

EXPLORE THE BEAUTIFUL ESTUARY OF MAWDDACH, WHICH WAS ONCE LACED WITH GOLD

WHERE	Mawddach Estuary, Gwynedd
STATS	←→ 10km (6¼ miles) one-way ②
START	Barmouth Harbour ⦿ SH614154
FINISH	George III Hotel, Penmaenpool ⦿ SH694184

Skim along the wide waters of Mawddach Estuary for a leisurely paddle in the heart of the Gwynedd countryside. The peaks of Snowdonia lie at your back as you head upstream. Forested inclines frame the water beautifully, particularly at sunrise or sunset. Running broadly southwest for 45km (28 miles), the River (Afon) Mawddach is famous for being one of Wales's last gold-mining areas. Although it is believed that all the gold has since disappeared from the estuary, that doesn't stop occasional gold-panners from chancing their arm.

Marvellous scenery aside, the Mawddach is also well known for historic pubs and hotels that enjoy enviable positions along its shores. The Mawddach fuses with the Irish Sea at Barmouth, where you'll find The Last Inn, a watering hole that dates back to the 15th century. At the end point, the George III Hotel at Penmaenpool has been providing thirsty visitors with real ale (and latterly food and accommodation) since 1650.

PADDLE THIS WAY

Start from the harbour at the seaside town of Barmouth. Weave between boats anchored near the shore and out into the Mawddach Estuary. Take time to look at the impressive line of arches that make up Barmouth Bridge, which carries a railway line. The estuary's extensive, sheltered mudflats are rich in marine worms, bivalves and crustaceans. Unseen by us, we often overlook their presence – noticing

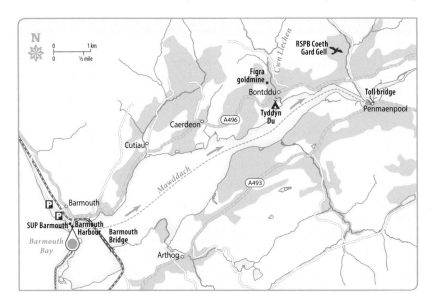

← Barmouth Harbour marks the start of a glorious paddle along the Mawddach Estuary. (SS)

instead the avian predators that feed upon them. Depending on the state of the tide, you may spot oystercatchers, grey herons and wildfowl including red-breasted merganser. A peregrine may coast overhead, keeping a lookout for an inattentive teal or other duck.

You are now heading upriver towards the sleepy village of Bontddu. If the crow were to fly from Bontddu to the seaside town of Barmouth, it would cover about 5km (3 miles). Your paddle may be longer depending on whether or not you skim the Mawddach's shores or glide along the river's central channel. Whichever you choose, you'll regale in magnificent views. Such scenery is pleasurable enough, but Mawddach also offers a fascinating history that, as you mosey around inquisitively, you may uncover.

Although Bontddu sits back from the water, its presence is marked by the Afon Cwn Llechen, a stream that flows into the estuary. Bontddu played a significant role in the local gold rush of the late 1800s. Were you to go ashore for a yomp in

↑ Suitably leashed up and wearing a personal flotation device (page 12). (Matt Breakwell/SUP Barmouth)

the nearby woods, you would find the remains of the waterwheel-powered Figra gold mine nestled within (♀ SH666190).

To your right (south), mountains greet the skyline; the peak of Cadair Idris, one of Wales's highest mountains, stands noticeably proud. The estuary now starts to narrow, accentuating the impact of your surroundings. Pastel-grey crags that flank both sides of the river form a sturdy and rugged backdrop that contrasts with the softer, greener foreground, lined with tall trees (indeed woodland that includes the RSPB nature reserve of Coed Garth Gell), plus small villages and a few scattered farms. Meanwhile, the floodplains along the immediate shoreline are a haven for wildlife in summer.

As you approach Penmaenpool you will see a white wooden-framed roadbridge that connects the banks of the River Mawddach (and the A roads that run along them). Pull ashore at the George III Hotel – and treat yourself to a well-earned drink. A pint of golden ale to mark a gold-medal paddle?

GETTING THERE

From Dolgellau, which lies at the junction of several A roads, take the A496 west to Barmouth. There are car parks off The Promenade at ♀ SH610156 and ♀ SH613158. Walk southeast to the harbour to launch. Nearest station is Barmouth on the Cambrian Coast Railway although it is a long way from the main line at Shrewsbury.

HIRE & LESSONS

SUP Barmouth (⟨ supbarmouth.co.uk) provides lessons and guided tours.

WHEN TO GO

Providing conditions are favourable this estuary is stunning at any time of year, but sunrise and sunset are particularly magnificent.

WHERE TO STAY & EAT

Near Bontddu, Tyddyn Du campsite (⟨ tyddyndu.webs.com) is a great option close to the estuary. In Barmouth, I love The Last Inn (⟨ last-inn.co.uk), a traditional pub with many original features. The pub's owners are also eradicating all single-use plastic, replacing it with biodegradable alternatives. What's not to like about that? In Penmaenpool, The George III Hotel (⟨ robinsonsbrewery.com/georgethethird) offers good local ales, food and accommodation.

TITBITS

Kayakers and canoeists can choose to retrace their route back to Penmaenpool. Paddleboarders should only do so if conditions are favourable.

28 BROADLY BRILLIANT

BECOME A 'FEN TIGER' AS YOU PADDLE TO NORFOLK'S BIGGEST BROAD

WHERE	Hickling Broad, Norfolk
STATS	↔ 11–15km (6¾–9⅓ miles) return ②
START/FINISH	Potter Heigham Bridge ♀ TG420185

Hickling Broad is the largest of all the broads in East Norfolk's 200km (125 miles) of network of largely navigable waterways. As natural as this biologically important wetland area may superficially appear, it is actually entirely manmade. The Norfolk Broads owe their existence to people digging for peat in medieval times. The pits left behind later flooded. The landscape that developed has become a national park.

Hickling Broad – used as a seaplane base during World War I – today encompasses just over 283 hectares of freshwater lake, marshes and reedbeds. The result is important habitat (largely protected by the Norfolk Wildlife Trust) for some of the UK's rarest wildlife. The stars include exciting birds (such as common crane, bittern and bearded tit), mammals (otter and water vole), and insects such as swallowtail (a butterfly) and Norfolk hawker (a dragonfly). In 2017, birdwatchers flocked to Potter Heigham Marshes, just south of Hickling, to see a breeding pair of black-winged stilts – a largely Mediterranean shorebird that seems poised to colonise Britain.

↑ A misty dawn on the River Thurne just east of Potter Heigham. (SS)

When entering Hickling Broad through a reed-lined channel, the sudden openness lends an impression of vastness. In two dimensions this may be true – but not the third, as the Broad is no deeper than 3m. Hickling's maze-like nooks and crannies form a trove of adventure demanding exploration. I particularly relish the fresh perspective brought by each little channel and the ample opportunities to discover wildlife. The longer you spend exploring, the easier it is to imagine yourself as a 'fen tiger' – a Broadland name both for the bittern and local people deriving a living from the waterways.

PADDLE THIS WAY

Start in the southern part of the village of Potter Heigham, which is a fairly busy boat-launching point. Enter the water either side of the medieval Potter Heigham Bridge, then travel downstream (eastnortheast) along the River Thurne. After you pass under the A149 roadbridge, this stretch of river is lined by small wooden houses, each one unique and (in its own way) charming.

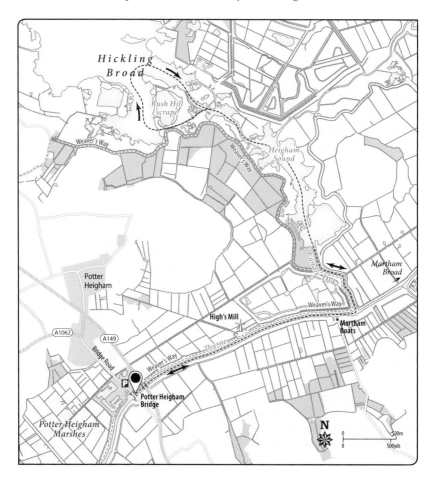

After you pass High's Mill on your left (north), the new reserve of Potter Heigham Marshes opens out on the same side. Although the wetlands themselves are largely hidden by a bank, you may spot birdwatchers on the towpath, scanning the lagoons' currently muddy shores, hoping to find rare birds. Just after you pass Martham Boats on the right (south), leave the Thurne, turning perpendicular to head north along a narrowed, reed-lined waterway called Candle Dyke.

This channel leads into Heigham Sound, this route's *pièce de résistance* for wildlife-watching. From now on, as you paddle along this hand-dug waterway, with channel markers either side of the shallows (be sure to stay in deeper water!), you could encounter fabulous animals anywhere.

Keep your eyes peeled for grey herons, cranes (which might announce their presence with a bugling cry) and bitterns (which fly over the reedbeds between feeding grounds). Great crested grebes frequent the open water, while marsh harriers quarter the tops of the reeds. A kingfisher may scoot past or a little egret may leap into the air. Along the banks look for Chinese water deer (which has vampire-like fangs). In the water itself, a v-shaped furrow may betray the presence of an otter swimming. A memorable midsummer encounter would be with a swallowtail, flying boldly on lacy wings of cream and black.

Keep paddling through Heigham Sound, passing the odd boat mooring before the channel opens up into the expanse of Hickling Broad. Explore its channels, circumnavigate the reedy island encasing Rush Hill scrape and cast your eye towards the distant horizons; can you glimpse the sea to the east? Once you're done, paddle back to your starting point at Potter Heigham.

GETTING THERE

From the A149/A1062 junction, head southeast along Bridge Road. Use the car park opposite Latham's shop just north of the River Thurne (TG419185), then launch from the adjacent Potter Heigham Bridge. By public transport, the most convenient route is to travel by train to North Walsham (which connects to mainline services at Norwich), then take bus 6 south to Potter Heigham.

HIRE & LESSONS

Norfolk Paddle Co (norfolkpaddleco.co.uk) offers guided tours and equipment hire for paddles on and around Hickling Broad. The company also runs Norfolk's main SUP club.

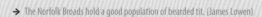

→ The Norfolk Broads hold a good population of bearded tit. (James Lowen)

WHERE TO STAY & EAT

Northwest of Hickling Broad (and a short drive from Potter Heigham) is the quirky Greyhound Inn (⊘ greyhoundinn.com) in Hickling, which has an excellent range of food and drink including locally brewed ales. A stone's throw from the launch/end point is BridgeStones of Potter (⊘ bridgestonesofpotter.co.uk).

TITBITS

Kayaks are suitable here as they can skip over the often vigorous aquatic plant growth. Paddleboarders should be more vigilant and either use smaller 'weed fins' or be prepared for the odd abrupt stop as vegetation catches the fin, pulling the board in one direction and sending you flying through the air in the other!

Also, although the water here is not that deep, it can be quite unnerving to the casual or unseasoned paddler when the wind blows, given that the Broads are quite exposed to the temperamental North Sea weather. This is where it is helpful to travel with a qualified guide.

↑ Paddling back into Potter Heigham after a relaxing excursion. (James Lowen)

29 MIDLANDS MAGIC

LEAP ABOARD FOR A TWO-DAY ADVENTURE ALONG ENGLAND'S THIRD-LONGEST RIVER, THE TRENT

WHERE	River Trent, Derbyshire/Nottinghamshire
STATS	↔ 50km (31 miles) one-way ⏳ 2–3 days ②
START	Trent Lock, Long Eaton ♀ SK490311
FINISH	Newark Castle, Newark-on-Trent ♀ SK795540

England's third-longest river (after the Thames and Severn), the Trent dominates the heart of the country. The Trent comes with an illustrious history too. Archaeological remains tell of Saxon villages, but greater significance is evident in its role as a transport 'highway' during the 19th-century industrialisation of the Midlands. Indeed, the Trent was a major working river until after World War II. With its heyday long gone, the Trent may still meander the same course but it does so largely unnoticed and underappreciated. It's time to pay homage to a great river.

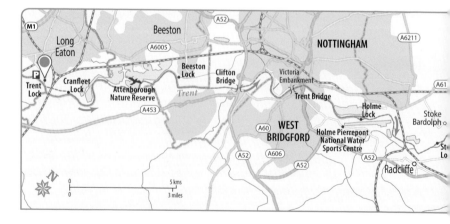

↑ The River Trent's sandy banks beyond Gunthorpe are the perfect place to cook your own breakfast. (Steve Bramall/S)

The hefty paddle from Trent Lock in Nottingham to Newark is a nod to the Trent's historic, natural and cultural relevance. It's a route of two halves. Upstream of Hazleford Lock is mostly scenic countryside with an abundance of wildlife. Downstream towards Newark, the paddle chimes a more historical tone as you pass through Newark locks to reach Newark Castle. Built in the 12th century, this fort came into its own during the English Civil War when it assumed strategic importance, controlling a principal route between northern and southern England.

PADDLE THIS WAY

Your launch view is admittedly inauspicious. As you put into the River Trent at Trent Lock, south of Long Eaton, the vista to the southeast is monopolised by a hulking power station. This may test your resolve, but don't let it deter you. Head east to swiftly enter peaceable countryside.

After 4km (2½ miles), the footpath to your left becomes shrouded by bankside trees. This luxuriant vegetation marks the start of Attenborough Nature Reserve. Birdwatchers, in particular, love Attenborough, which runs beyond the left (north) side of the river for just over 3km (1¾ miles). In summer there are colonies of common tern and sand martin, while winter brings waterfowl such as great crested grebe and goldeneye, plus bitterns (a type of heron camouflaged to blend in with its reedbed habitat). Summer also sees the air fill with butterflies (including brown argus) and dragonflies. There's something for everyone here.

Spotting wildlife from the solitude and stillness of the water is special. Being on a paddleboard separates you from human hubris. This magnifies the sounds of nature – birds chirping, trees rustling in the wind, swans preparing to take flight. A real feast for the senses.

Past the tranquillity that infuses Attenborough, the landscape becomes more urban as the public footpath reappears. Buildings, graffiti-marked bridges and people signal your approach to Nottingham's Victoria Embankment. If you need

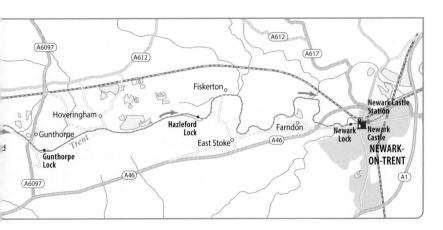

any reassurance with your bearings, you should soon see the iconic Trent Bridge. Perhaps Nottingham's most famous landmark, it sits at the heart of Nottingham's sporting district, lending its name to one of England's biggest and most famous cricket grounds.

Reaching Trent Bridge marks 10km from the start point. It would be rude not to take advantage of mooring options along the bridge and then refuel at one of the waterside bars. Southbank Bar, for example, serves ales from nearby Navigation Brewery.

A further 3km (1¾ miles) downstream, you reach Holme Pierrepont, which sits on the right (south). This is home to the National Water Sports Centre and British Canoeing – a place of quasi-pilgrimage for anyone for whom a paddle is a natural extension of their arm. Here you will need to portage Holme Lock.

After Holme Pierrepont, the Trent meanders considerably. After 4km (2½ miles), Radcliffe's impressive rust-coloured cliffs grab your attention. In summer they may be largely concealed by overgrowth of trees and shrubbery, but as autumn evolves they become far more prominent. Formed from Triassic red shale, the cliffs tower above the water to your right (south), contrasting with the vast, open, rolling expanse of green on the left (north).

As you pass Stoke Bardolph, willows and other lush vegetation drape over the river. The quietness attracts anglers, but so too water voles (immortalised as Ratty in Kenneth Grahame's *The Wind in the Willows*). Look along the water line for signs of their tunnelling. If you don't glimpse these shy creatures, you should at least see grey heron, coot and moorhen.

Some 5km (3 miles) beyond Stoke Bardolph, the small village of Gunthorpe sits on the left (north) of the river. It marks the halfway point in the journey. This milestone may prompt you into replenishing energy levels at a waterside restaurant or café. I particularly recommend Biondi Bistro, where staff are extremely helpful and the cake is excellent.

Beyond Gunthorpe Lock lies a stretch of 6km (3¾ miles) to Hazleford Lock. Mid-river sits an enticing, secluded small island with an old cottage. Other than from the river, access is solely by a gated footbridge. This smidgeon of land presents a perfect spot for wild camping. If you are suitably equipped and briefed (page 11), consider adjourning here for the night. What better way to drift to sleep than with the soothing sound of water from lock and weir?

You are now on the home straight. The river remains wide and, despite scattered industrial areas and the odd distant power station, you are largely flanked by sweeping countryside. The Bromley marks your arrival in the village of Fiskerton, 3km (1¾ miles) from Gunthorpe. If you are paddling by at breakfast time, you might regret that this riverside pub doesn't open for a few hours yet. If so, pull up at a sandy bank just beyond Fiskerton – and cook your own fry-up.

Some 4km (2½ miles) on, you reach Farndon on the right (south). Farndon Boathouse is one of a couple of local gastropubs that may call your name – though be aware that the riverside garden gets busy on warm days. Departing Farndon, pass by a marina bulging with boats. The remaining 15km (9⅓ miles) largely comprises farmland and pasture. Cows grazing by the riverbank peer at you curiously as you paddle alongside them. Throw in sheep and horses, and you will really feel in the heart of the British countryside.

From around 5km (3 miles) before Newark-on-Trent, the bucolic vistas are gradually replaced by urbanised, residential terrain. Rather than regret the dissolution of rurality, embrace a historical perspective. Newark was once an important inland port. The former wharves and warehouses – which once stored wool, coal, grain and timber – now serve as cafés or riverside apartments. Reflect on their previous lives as you paddle past to reach Newark Lock.

The lock is significant for two reasons. The first is obvious: it marks your entry into the heart of the town and the end of the paddle. The second is unexpected. As the lock opens, the view ahead genuinely takes you aback. The stone walls of Newark Castle – the true gem of this journey – tumble into the Trent. The view from the water is breathtaking.

Newark is popular with boaters, so there are plenty of places to moor up. Explore the castle, with its walls, dungeons and even quiet garden areas. Celebrate your journey along the Trent by ascending the ramparts and looking back west along the river, reflecting on what you have achieved.

↑ The iconic Trent Bridge, Nottingham. (Will Robson/S)

Newark Castle: a fitting culmination to a mighty paddle. (Ingvar Tjostheim/S)

GETTING THERE

Leave the M1 at junction 24a, and take the A50 west to the first roundabout. Come off here, heading northeast along the B6540 to Long Eaton. Take the first right after you cross the River Trent, and follow Lock Lane to Trent Lock car park (⌖ tinyurl.com/trent-lock), where you launch. There are train stations at either end of the route (Long Eaton and Newark-on-Trent). From the former, it is a short taxi ride to the start. There are direct trains between the stations, so it is easy to get back to your vehicle at the end of the paddle.

HIRE & LESSONS

There are no suitable local providers so you'll need your own equipment. If you want lessons locally, you could do worse than visit the National Water Sports Centre at Holme Pierrepont (⌖ nwscnotts.com).

WHERE TO STAY & EAT

My favourite suggestions for eateries along the route are Southbank Bar (in Nottingham: ⌖ southbankbar.co.uk), Biondi Bistro (Gunthorpe: ⌖ biondibistro.co.uk), The Bromley (Fiskerton: ⌖ bromleyatfiskerton.com) and Farndon Boathouse (Farndon: ⌖ farndonboathouse.co.uk). In terms of accommodation, wild camping (page 11) is the most convenient option, but there is a formal campsite at Holme Pierrepont (⌖nwscnotts.com/nwsc/camping-pitches). If you want a bed, the Unicorn Hotel (⌖ unicornhotelpub.co.uk) at Gunthorpe is conveniently located and there is ample accommodation in Nottingham.

TITBITS

Two words of warning. Inexperienced paddlers should allow time for a more leisurely journey over three days. There are some exposed stretches of water that, if the conditions are against you (eg: a headwind), can be tiring and will slow you down considerably. Err on the side of caution. Second, should you fancy continuing beyond Newark, be aware that at Cromwell Weir (10km/6¼ miles on), the River Trent turns tidal – and is for experienced paddlers only.

30 LITTLE ITALY

AN ESTUARINE PADDLE PAST A LONG WHITE STRAND TO THE UNIQUE VILLAGE OF PORTMEIRION

WHERE	Black Rock Sands, Gwynedd
STATS	←→ 11.5km (7¼ miles) return ③
START/FINISH	Car park, Black Rock Sands ♀ SH543364

While its name may conjure thoughts of a dark, stony beach, the reality of Gwynedd's Black Rock Sands could hardly be more different. This strand is wide, pale and sandy; its moniker derives from the large, shadowy rocks, caves and pools that mark its northern border.

The beach might be reason enough for this paddle, but throw in the cute coastal villages of Borth-y-Gest and Porthmadog, and you're on to a winner. Even then, we're not done. Further up the estuary lies

↑ The beach at Borth-y-Gest overlooks the paddle route. (SS)

this route's ultimate treat: the quirky, Italian-style village of Portmeirion. Designed and built from scratch by architect Sir Clough Williams-Ellis over 50 years from 1925, the village has become one of Wales's top tourist attractions, attracting 225,000 visitors annually. With colourful buildings and unexpected vistas, Portmeirion is as unmissable as it is unique.

PADDLE THIS WAY

Launch from Black Rock Sands and head east. Directly ahead, in the distance, the Snowdonian range adds depth to the vista. To your left, an expansive caravan site washes the slopes. As you enter the estuary of the River (Afon) Glaslyn, bear northeast, keeping Harlech Point well to your right (south).

To your left, the village of Borth-y-Gest peeks out from the coastline. Set further back to the north is Porthamdog, from which the Ffestiniog railway beavers east. You are heading for the headland that splits the estuary and behind which the village of Portmeirion shelters. A clandestine cove of fine white sand seeks to greet you, but follow the promontory eastwards as it becomes shrouded in verdant woodland. Soon the pastel-coloured buildings of Portmeirion reveal themselves stacked up the hillside. Pull up if you fancy exploring. And you should – there really is nothing like Portmeirion anywhere in Britain.

Further east, the small island of Ynys Gifftan demands your attention. And this despite its diminutive stature – barely 40m high – in comparison with the craggy peaks bossing the backdrop. At low tide, you can reach Ynys Gifftan (carefully!) on foot. But better to paddle around it, I say. There is not much to investigate on the island itself – a single dilapidated cottage – so circumnavigate and retrace the route to the start.

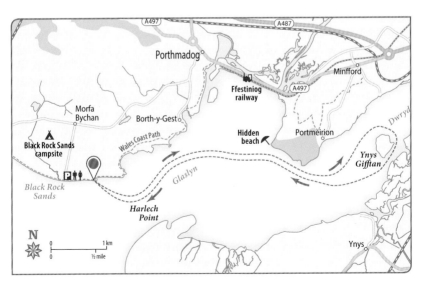

GETTING THERE

Leave the A487 at Porthmadog, cross the town and head southwest along minor roads to Morfa Bychan. Turn south here to use the car park on the beach (literally!) at ♥ SH543364. Avoid parking too close to the high-water mark as cars have floated off into the blue... Launch from the beach. Nearest train station is Aberystwyth, from where you can catch the 99 bus to Capel Nazareth then walk 25 minutes to the beach.

HIRE & LESSONS

No hire company services this stretch of coastline so you will require your own equipment.

WHERE TO STAY & EAT

Affordable, accessible camping is at Black Rock Sands campsite (⊘ blackrocksands.webs.com). Portmeirion village has a few places to stay and eat (⊘ portmeirion-village.com).

TITBITS

Given expansive mud at low tide, this is a paddle best done at high tide. Bear in mind that winds can sweep you out to sea.

Ready, steady, launch! Kayaking at Black Rock Sands. (Kevin Richardson/A)

31 THE STREAM IN THE SKY

TAKE THE AERIAL ROUTE ALONG THE LLANGOLLEN CANAL, FORTY METRES ABOVE GROUND

WHERE	Llangollen Canal, Denbighshire
STATS	↔ 6km (4 miles) return, depending how far you go one-way ③
START/FINISH	Pontcysyllte Aqueduct car park ♀ SJ270422

One of just three World Heritage Sites in Wales, Pontcysyllte Aqueduct is the UK's highest (39m) and longest (307m) such construct. Made from cast iron and stone, this 18-arch structure was completed in 1805 so the 18 arches could carry the Llangollen Canal over the Dee Valley. Its grand scale is impressive to the point of intimidation – a fabulous place for paddling amid panoramic views over the surrounding montane Area of Outstanding National Beauty and over the valley below. (Just don't look down if you have a thing about heights…) This route travels just a short section of the Llangollen Canal, but if you were to follow it east, you would cross from Wales into England.

PADDLE THIS WAY

Start from the Pontcysyllte Aqueduct car park, and launch through a suitable gap between narrowboats moored along the edge. To your northeast, a shrubby verge marks the northernmost extent of the Llangollen Canal. Turn southwest and pass below a small footbridge. Within 50m, you commence the incredible

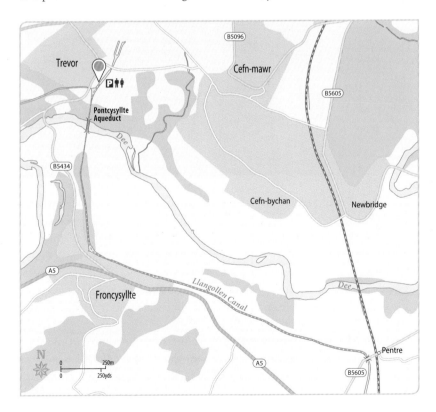

← Yes, you really can paddle through the sky, thanks to Pontcysyllte Aqueduct. (Aigars Mellitis/D)

crossing over Pontcysyllte Aqueduct. For 300 glorious metres, savour unparalleled views as this feat of engineering floats you high above the River Dee, over fields scattered with cattle and a wooded canopy exhibiting many shades of green.

The scenery – particularly with mountains on the skyline – is undeniably impressive. But what will strike you most is the aqueduct's serenity. Even the presence of a footpath running alongside the canal does not detract from the acute sense of separation from the world. For an enchanting, if short, time, you feel as if you were gliding through the air.

The transition from air back to land is seamless, as trees return to your line of sight and houses appear on the banks of the canal. What follows is a pleasant paddle through winding Welsh countryside. Take opportunities to peer through the shrubby hedgerows and you will see sheep grazing peaceably in verdant fields.

↑ The aerial waterway of Pontcysyllte Aqueduct. (Lizzie Carr)

Around 1km (⅔ mile) after the aqueduct, a footbridge crosses low over the canal. It's only a metre wide, so the best option is to portage round it. Slightly inconvenient, but no more than that. At this point you flank the village of Froncysyllte, where there are a few eateries should you be hungry now or on the return. The next 1.5km (1 mile) or so is largely wooded, with green pasture to your left (north) and – hidden from view but sometimes within earshot – the A5 road to your right (south).

Explore to your heart's content. As there are no tides to consider on a canal, you can drag this route out for as long as you wish (the route on the map takes you as far as the B5605 roadbridge at Pentre). When you've had enough, simply retrace your 'steps'. Were you to time it right, reaching the aqueduct at sunset would make for a very fine experience – a gentle paddle through the sky as you watch the sun slowly drop below the horizon. Perfection on a paddleboard.

GETTING THERE

Some 10km (6¼ miles) south of Wrexham, turn off the A483, heading west on the A5. After 3.5km (2¼ miles), turn north along the B5434, following signs for Pontcysyllte Aqueduct car park (pontcysyllte-aqueduct.co.uk) in Trevor village. Nearest train stations are Ruabon or Chirk, from where you can walk or taxi the 2km (1¼ miles) to the launch point.

HIRE & LESSONS

Ty Nant Outdoors (tynantoutdoors.com) rents paddleboards and offers lessons on the Llangollen Canal and within the Dee Valley.

WHEN TO GO

There are no seasonal constraints (being tide-free), so any time of year is suitable. Time of day is a more important consideration: paddling over the aqueduct at sunrise and sunset is both quieter and particularly awe-inspiring.

WHERE TO STAY & EAT

If you need food or a bed, you could do worse than choose the Queen's Hotel in Cefn-mawr (www.queenshotelpontcysyllte.co.uk), a charming 17th-century establishment.

TITBITS

Although most of the route is sheltered, Pontcysyllte Aqueduct can feel pretty wobbly if it is windy, so check conditions before heading out. Safety is paramount here, given that there is no barrier on one side of the aqueduct. I recommend waiting for calmer weather. If you must paddle, then I suggest being seated or kneeling and ensure there is no oncoming traffic.

32 LET'S TWIST AGAIN

EXPERIENCED PADDLERS WILL RELISH THE MEANDERS ALONG THE BORDER BETWEEN WALES & ENGLAND

WHERE	Bangor-on-Dee, Clwyd
STATS	←→ 24km (15 miles) one-way ③
START	Bangor Bridge, Bangor-on-Dee ♀ SJ387453
FINISH	Farndon ♀ SJ412545

The River Dee is a properly British river, flowing through areas of both Wales and England. Indeed, in places (including the home stretch on this route), it marks the border that separates the rule of Cardiff from that of Westminster.

The section between Bangor-on-Dee and Farndon is one of the most remote and peaceful stretches of river I have ever paddled. This paddle isn't about historic landmarks, obscure wildlife or people-watching. It is about extracting yourself from the world and immersing yourself in unstinting remoteness. Most of the time there is barely a building or person in sight.

The route is also splendidly winding and deliciously meandering – nearly thrice as long over the water as the proverbial crow would fly. As you twist through the Dee's charms, be cautious of the river's extreme tidal range. For the more experienced paddler, it's an adventure playground (and there are more rapids nearby; see *Adrenaline junkies*, page 159); for the novice, they are nevertheless best avoided. Indeed, this extreme tidal range cautions against the inexperienced following this route (see *Titbits*, page 158).

PADDLE THIS WAY

Launch from the small shingle beach just south of the bridge at Bangor-on-Dee, preferably at high tide and taking the ebb down (north). Miles of sweeping

↑ Farndon – Holt Bridge – the end point for this paddle. (UK City Images/A)

countryside – farmland, pasture and open, grassy fields – set the tone for this journey.

There are 13 long meanders along this route, and counting them is a good way of keeping track of your progress. As you reach the sixth meander, around 4.5km (2¾ miles) from the start, you'll confront a section of miniature rapids. The next 3km (1¾ miles) are sprinkled with mildly white water before the river quietens, and returns to the calmer, but still brisk, paddle of previously.

Paddling 24km (15 miles) in a day is a big ask by any stretch of the imagination, especially if the wind is working against you. Although there are no formal camping spots on this route, there are sandy bays, low verges and quiet corners of fields that would be perfect to sensitively pitch a tent for the night, leaving at sunrise the following morning. Try and plan ahead, and seek permission to camp at your intended stopover site (page 11 offers advice on wild-camping etiquette).

Continue paddling north towards the village of Farndon. As you draw 'level' with Shocklach Green you'll be crossing the border from Wales into England. For the final 10km (6¼ miles) towards Farndon, the steep sides of the river gradually become dotted with houses. Being set back slightly from the river, however, these do not intrude on the sense of isolation.

As you pass under the A534 to enter Holt, you will see on your left (west) the remains of Holt Castle, which lies inside a quarry believed to have provided stone for the fort's construction. This fort was built between 1282 and 1311 by order of King Llywelyn the Last, the first Prince of Wales, to guard the river crossing now occupied by the beautifully arched Holt–Farndon Bridge, 800m (½ mile) downstream. The remains are hard to decipher as almost all stonework was removed in the 16th century.

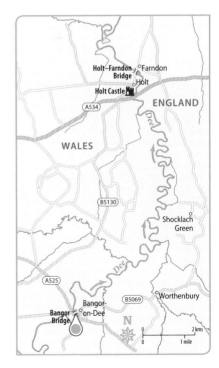

Continue past the castle, round the bend to reach Farndon, marked by buildings appearing on the right (east) bank of the river. Pull up at the Holt–Farndon Bridge and congratulate yourself on a long paddle neatly completed. You could return by river (perhaps the next day), book a taxi to take you back to the launch point or – with planning – travel with a friend and leave a car at either end.

GETTING THERE

Bangor-on-Dee is off the A525, 6km (4 miles) southeast of Wrexham. Park along High Street. Walk west to the bridge adjacent to the Royal Oak pub, climb over a low stone wall and walk to the Dee's east bank to launch. Nearest train station is Wrexham (although Chester may be more convenient), from where you can take bus 146 for 15 minutes to Bangor-on-Dee.

HIRE & LESSONS

Based on Anglesey (a bit distant, admittedly), Psyched Paddleboarding (psychedpaddleboarding.com) offers guided tours in North Wales.

WHERE TO STAY & EAT

In Bangor-on-Dee, The Royal Oak (theroyaloakbangorondee.co.uk) offers good food and drink. The Buck House (thebuckhousebangorondee.co.uk) also offers overnight accommodation as well as food and drink. Alternatively, wild-camp (page 11).

TITBITS

The River Dee has an extremely high tidal range and can be tough in harsh conditions, and after heavy rainfall. Only experienced paddlers should attempt to complete this route. Moreover, at low water, particularly after dry weather, you may run into the ground in some

areas. But don't worry too much; it shouldn't take long for you to find enough water to get going again. There is useful guidance on this stretch of river at ⚘ tinyurl.com/dee-paddle.

ADRENALINE JUNKIES

The River Dee (aka Afon Dyfrdwy) has a split personality. Away from the largely calm waters of this agreeably benign waterway, there are gnarly white waters too. Perfect for experienced paddlers (particularly those in kayaks or canoes) . . . if you dare!

From Serpent's Tail – as uninviting as it sounds and responsible for upskittling many an experienced paddler – to Horseshoe Falls and Llangollen town weir there are exciting sections of the Dee that draw in thrill-seekers from afar.

If you're of the adrenaline-junkie mould, you're probably already chomping at the bit. If not, then also there for the taking (indeed, your taking) are rapids including Boulder Blast and Tombstones, whose names make them sound remarkably like exhilarating theme-park rides and that wouldn't be far wrong!

These are tough but playful features where rapids meet you in quick succession. You'll need to take care of yourself at each – but, at Llangollen town weir you need to take care of the site too. Although you'll probably be too busy concentrating on staying afloat to be looking out for Atlantic salmon, freshwater pearl mussel and otter, they live here – and their habitat needs respecting. Much of the River Dee is of conservation importance. Please be mindful of this on your paddles and avoid disturbing the habitat.

Llangollen town weir offers an exhilarating extension to the route for experienced paddlers.

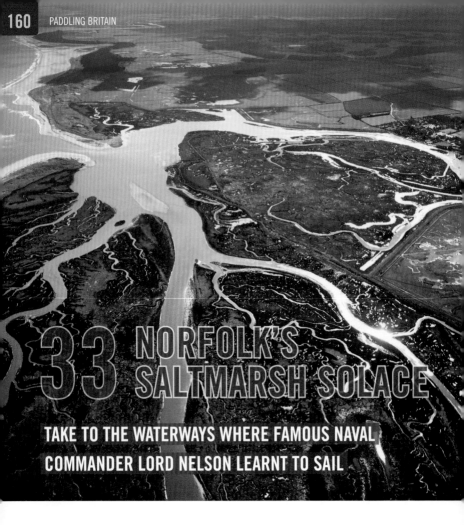

33 NORFOLK'S SALTMARSH SOLACE

TAKE TO THE WATERWAYS WHERE FAMOUS NAVAL COMMANDER LORD NELSON LEARNT TO SAIL

WHERE	Deepdale Marshes, Norfolk
STATS	←→ 8km (5 miles) one-way ②
START	Harbour Way, Brancaster Staithe ♀ TF792444
FINISH	East Harbour Way, Burnham Overy Staithe ♀ TF845444

The beauty of North Norfolk for paddlers is the maze-like marsh system that connects land with the open water of its sweeping coastlines. Located west of centre, Scolt Head Island is a marvel. This offshore barrier island is separated from the mainland by a narrow channel; it was originally a spit formed by longshore drift. Bought by the National Trust in 1923, Scolt Head swiftly became a National Nature Reserve and part of the Norfolk Coast Area of Outstanding Natural Beauty. Paddling is the perfect way to enjoy the island while causing the least amount of interference to the environment.

Despite being a mere 6.5km (4 miles) long, Scolt Head is home to a considerable variety of birds thanks to a diversity of habitats that includes shingle, mud, sand flat, dune and saltmarsh. In summer, this low

↑ A migrant bird's-eye view of the saltmarsh venation of Burnham Overy Staithe. (SS)

island hosts an important colony of Sandwich and little terns, while other seasons see flocks of brent geese, with their evocative, rippling calls, plus waders such as redshank and curlew, which throng to rich feeding grounds on its tidal reaches.

Life along this stretch of the East Anglian coast is all about the sea. Fishermen pride themselves in harvesting Brancaster mussels (served up in local eateries) and various harbours hum with yacht-based activity. North Norfolk also has a strong nautical history. Famous naval commander Admiral Horatio Lord Nelson was born nearby at Burnham Thorpe and first got to grips with sailing at Burnham Overy Staithe. Another local seafarer was Captain Richard Woodget, who skippered the sailing clipper *Cutty Sark*; he grew up in Burnham Norton. Us waterborne folk are in good company in this part of Norfolk.

PADDLE THIS WAY

Launch from Brancaster Staithe Harbour, ideally on a westerly and an hour before high tide so that the incoming water propels your journey. Head northeast, briefly joining Mow Creek, before reaching the entrance of Norton Creek, which you should follow east. Here you will see a wide expanse of marshland on your right (south) and the sandy shores of Scolt Head Island on your left (north).

At the west (Brancaster Staithe) end of Scolt Head Island you'll notice landmarks such as the small wooden huts used by National Trust wardens. The island is a haven for breeding terns, which thrive in the absence of disturbance by people. As you paddle east along Norton Creek, parallel with the Peddars Way and North Norfolk Coastal Path on the mainland, the old windmill of Burnham Overy Staithe cleaves into view on your right. Set back from the coast on a slight incline (there's not much in the way of hills in this part of Norfolk), this six-storey tower mill dates back to 1816. Two centuries on, it now serves as a holiday let.

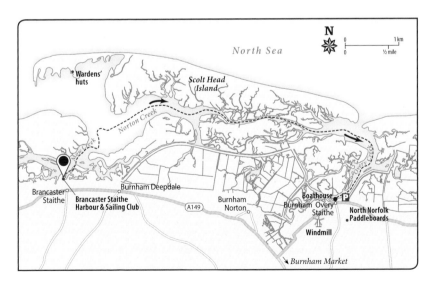

GETTING THERE

The start and finish points are both immediately north of the A149 that runs along the North Norfolk coast. You can park along Harbour Way opposite Brancaster Staithe Sailing Club (⊘ bssc.net; ♥ TF791442), at the entrance to the harbour. You can also park on firm land by the harbour itself – but be warned that any tide over 8.3m will flood the harbour area – and possibly your vehicle too. Alternatively, there is informal parking in the layby along the A149 just west of Brancaster Staithe at ♥ TF788442. The car park (♥ TF844443) at Burnham Overy Staithe Harbour – where you finish – also floods on tides over 8.4m. The Coasthopper bus runs between Hunstanton and Sheringham, so it's easy to get back to Brancaster Staithe. You can connect at Hunstanton for a bus to King's Lynn. There are trains from King's Lynn to Cambridge/London, and from Sheringham to Norwich.

HIRE & LESSONS

In Burnham Overy Staithe, North Norfolk Paddleboards (⊘ northnorfolkpaddleboards.co.uk) rents boards and equipment, and offers guided tours.

WHEN TO GO

While summer is always a good season for paddling (sunshine, long hours of daylight), autumn would be a good bet if you fancy a spot of birdwatching alongside your waterborne excursion.

↑ When paddling around Brancaster Staithe, take care to avoid other users of the waterway. (Greg Balfour Evans/A)

About 5km (3 miles) along the channel, turn right (south) into Overy Creek, which leads to Burnham Overy Staithe. As you do so, look left (east). Facing the eastern tip of Scolt Head you can see Gun Hill, which marks the westernmost extent of Burnham Overy Dunes. This dune system, smattered with dense scrubland, is famous among birdwatchers for attracting good numbers of migrant birds. This is particularly true in autumn when rare warblers such as yellow-browed may excite the binocular-toting crowd. More likely to be seen are thrushes such as redwing and flocks of goldcrest (Britain's joint-smallest bird).

Continue roughly southwest for 1km (⅔ mile) to reach Burnham Overy Staithe Harbour. Hugging the bank on your left (the east), head for the black-and-white boathouse. You may see lots of walkers out enjoying this area, and you may spot even more birdwatchers – particularly between autumn and spring, when the muddy areas host waders such as turnstone, bar-tailed godwit and knot.

As you approach the harbour, be careful of the groynes. They are marked with green buoys so should be easy to spot. If paddleboarding, your fin may catch these if the tide is low or if you get too close. Finish on the sandy shores of the harbour in Burnham Overy Staithe. If that was thirsty work, why not head to the village local, The Hero, just up the road from the harbour?

WHERE TO STAY & EAT

Norfolk's renowned mussels are harvested at Brancaster, so feature on many a local menu. In Burnham Overy Staithe, The Hero is an excellent pub, refurbished in 2016 (⊘ theheroburnhamovery.co.uk). In Brancaster Staithe The Jolly Sailors is an award-winning family pub (⊘ jollysailorsbrancaster.co.uk). Between the two villages, at Burnham Deepdale, is the Deepdale Café (⊘ deepdale-cafe.co.uk), a favourite among walkers. At the same location is Deepdale Backpackers, an independent hostel that also offers camping (⊘ deepdalebackpackers.co.uk). The nearby small town of Burnham Market, while quite fancy, has several accommodation options.

TITBITS

One village west of Brancaster Staithe is Brancaster. The bay north of the village – appropriately called Brancaster Bay – is a popular SUP surf spot when the weather isn't playing ball for a gentle paddle. To get there, drive north along Broad Lane to the public car park opposite Royal West Norfolk Golf Club (♀ TF771451). Walk 100m to the beach and jump in! The Magic Seaweed (⊘ magicseaweed.com) surf report for Cromer Beach serves as a very good indication of what is happening further west at Brancaster.

→ Look for bar-tailed godwit as you paddle Norfolk's creeks. (James Lowen)

34 SNOWDONIAN SECRET

FLEE SNOWDONIA'S TOURIST CROWDS BY PADDLING A LAKE AT THE MIGHTY MOUNTAIN'S BASE

WHERE	Llyn Padarn, Gwynedd
STATS	←→ 8km (5 miles) round trip ②
START/FINISH	Snowdonia Watersports 📍SH573609

I t's time to immerse yourself in the rugged surroundings of world-renowned Snowdonia. Like many of this area's lakes, Llyn Padarn owes its existence to the passage of a glacier. At just over 3km (2 miles) long, it is among the largest. Being situated at the northwest foot of Mt Snowdon itself renders it among the most picturesque. However, unlike other lakes, Padarn is largely sheltered – which is a very good thing for a paddler. It also benefits from a unique assemblage of interest features, notably a train line that runs parallel with the lake, a slate museum on its banks, and a famous tree that is honoured with its very own Facebook page. However many times you paddle Padarn, there is always something new to discover.

Fed by the River (Afon) Rhythallt, Llyn Padarn fronts Llanberis, the village that serves as the most popular departure point for a hike up to the summit of Mt Snowdon. But what proportion of the visitors to this delightful community – all intent on scaling the montane heights – consider a rather different way of exploring? Imagine staring up towards Snowdon's peak from the middle of the lake that sits underneath it with nothing within earshot bar the swishing of water and the odd swan taking to the air on whooshing wings. No droves of tourists racing past to reach the trig pillar marking Snowdon's crest. Just you and the views. If that doesn't tickle your fancy then nothing will.

PADDLE THIS WAY

Opposite Snowdonia Watersports there is a public car park, by which lies a jetty that is perfect for entering the water. Once waterborne, paddle northwest to the

↑ Llyn Padarn: a lake free of Snowdonia's maddening crowds. (Gail Johnson/S)

head of Llyn Padarn, staying close to the left (west) shore. You'll pass The Lone Tree shortly after you set off. The tree is exactly as its name suggests – a short, solitary tree, usually set out in the water. In peak season, you'll usually find a gaggle of tourists queuing to get a picture of it.

Keep going northwest, the western shore to your left. After 2km (1¼ miles), the deciduous woodland lining the banks breaks to reveal Craig yr Undeb. This

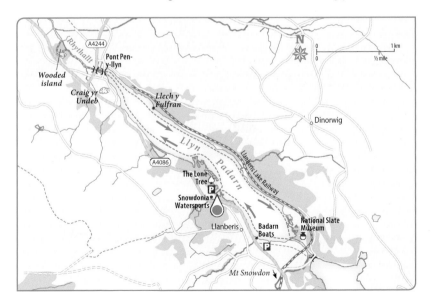

crag is now favoured by climbers, but its role in 1874 was somewhat different. The name means 'Union Rock', and it was the locus for the inaugural (and clandestine) meeting of the North Wales Quarrymen's Union.

After about 2.2km (1⅓ miles), you reach the lake head. Here there is a bridge (Pont Pen-y-llyn), probably with a few swans going about their business. Pass underneath the bridge, then under a second (this one transporting the A4244). You are now on the River (Afon) Rhythallt, which feeds into Llyn Padarn.

After about 500m (⅓ mile) you come across a tiny, heavily wooded island. Go round it, whether clockwise or anticlockwise (your call). The eastern channel around the island is very narrow. If there has been little recent rainfall, it may not be navigable. But don't let that stop you: whether board under your arm or kayak on your back, you'll find a way.

Once you have circumnavigated the island, return southeast along the Rhythallt. Pass back under both bridges, then hug the shore on your left (north). About 800m (½ mile) along you'll come across a rocky outcrop called Llech y

↑ There is a lot to explore on Llyn Padarn, so go equipped for a full day of fun. (Stephenmeese/S)

Fulfran, which marks the halfway point in the route. Find a spot to take a breath and enjoy the craggy mountain views of surrounding Snowdonia to the south. Don't rush. Grant yourself a moment to take it all in. When you are ready, and only when, journey on.

Having regained your puff race the Llanberis Lake Railway narrow-gauge steam train that chugs along the northern shore – and wave back at any kids gesticulating excitedly at you. Continue a further 3.5km (2 miles) to the head of the lake, where you'll see the National Slate Museum set back behind the treeline. Weave your way through rowing boats that visitors have hired from Badarn Boats and enter the final straight.

Push hard to the finish and if the wind isn't at your back – as it was when I completed this route – you'll need to press even harder, round the final spit of land and the jetty will come upon you. If conditions are calm, however, the stillness transforms the lake into a watery mirror that perfectly reflects Snowdonia's skyline, trees and mountains. A thrilling paddle completed.

GETTING THERE

Access to Llyn Padarn is from the A4086, 1km (⅔ mile) northwest of Llanberis. Use the car park opposite (north of) Snowdonia Watersports (◉ SH573609). Launch from the adjacent jetty. Nearest train station is Bangor, from where buses 85/86 run to Llanberis (◈ gwynedd.gov.uk/timetables).

HIRE & LESSONS

Snowdonia Watersports (◈ snowdoniawatersports.com) rents equipment and kit and offers guided sessions on Llyn Padarn. Other facilities include a place to leave valuables, changing room (modest charge payable if you are not a customer) and a small café.

WHERE TO STAY & EAT

No trip to Llanberis is complete without a visit to the famous Pete's Eats (◈ petes-eats.co.uk), a brightly coloured café that has fed hearty grub to hungry walkers since 1978. Full Welsh breakfasts with massive mugs of tea to wash it down are a favourite. There's always a great buzz. For immediate refuelling after you come off the water, the café at Snowdonia Watersports (see above) is convenient. Llanberis (◈ llanberis. com) is a tourist hotspot so has no shortage of B&Bs and hotels. Check Airbnb (◈ airbnb.com) for some alternatives: I have stayed in some wonderful homes with great views of both mountains and lake.

TITBITS

Llyn Padarn is beautiful and tranquil. If that's your thing, why not explore another (even quieter) paddle spot nearby? Head to Llynnau Mymbyr – smaller than Padarn and even less touristy – which is 19km (12 miles east, near Capel Curig).

35 MEDIEVAL MAGIC

BRAVE CONWY'S CHOPPY WATERS TO ADMIRE A WORLD HERITAGE SITE CASTLE

WHERE	Conwy Bay, Conwy
STATS	←→ 8km (5 miles) round trip ③
START/FINISH	Conwy Morfa Beach car park ♀ SH762787

The Irish Sea greets the north coast of Wales at Conwy Bay, offering a fabulous open-water paddle that pushes upstream into the Conwy River to arrive at Conwy Castle. This fort is one of Britain's finest surviving medieval castles, built by Edward I in the 13th century during his conquest of Wales. It is now one of just six World Heritage Sites in Wales (another being Pontcysyllte Aqueduct, page 152).

Everything about Conwy oozes tradition. The wooden shack selling candyfloss. The old red phone boxes standing to attention below the castle's stone wall. The fishing pots and trawler nets awaiting their next trip out to sea.

PADDLE THIS WAY

Launch from Conwy Morfa Beach, a mighty expanse of pale sand backed by unspoilt green hills. To the south, inland, Snowdonia National Park contains the source of the Conwy River. To the west is the island of Anglesey. Paddle east towards the entrance to the Conwy River, staying close to the right (south) shore. This curves inland, forsaking coast for river and heading upstream past a quay crammed with yachts and sailing boats.

↑ Haul ashore at the beach by Conwy Castle to visit the famous fort. (Lukasz Pajor/S)

Straight ahead, about 800m (½ mile) upstream, a small headland of Bondlondeb Wood protrudes into the Conwy River from the right (now the west). As you reach Conwy Quay, identified by moored boats and a low stone wall that leads out into the shoreline, you will see two remarkable buildings.

First, Conwy Castle sits majestically next to the Conwy Suspension Bridge – grand and imposing, with eight round towers. Second, and suitably contrasting, is Britain's smallest house, a vividly scarlet 16th-century fisherman's cottage on the waterfront road of Lower Gate Street. Just 1.8m (6 feet) wide, its two rooms are open for visiting (⌂ thesmallesthouse.co.uk; ⊙ Mar–Oct).

If you pass under the bridge and follow the shore round to the right (west), you'll find a small shingle beach below the castle grounds on the south side of the channel. Why not pull your board up and rest? If you have time, it's also worth wandering around Conwy town, which you can access from the harbour. Plenty of places sell fresh local fish, which you might nibble on a quayside bench (just mind out for hungry gulls) – before gliding back downstream on the exiting tide (if you time it right).

If you want to mix things up on the paddle back (as the map suggests) then head from the castle to the opposite (east) side of the river before paddling downstream. You will pass Deganwy Quay Marina and Deganwy Beach before journeying back west across the river, returning to your start point of Conwy Morfa Beach.

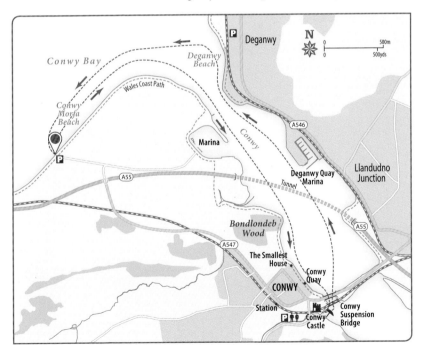

Conwy River, leading north into Conwy Bay. (SS)

GETTING THERE

Leave the A55 at junction 17 and take the minor roads north then west for 500m (⅓ mile) to reach the car park at Conwy Morfa Beach. Then, simply walk to the shore to launch. Nearest train station is Conwy, from where you can walk 2.5km (1½ miles) to Conwy Morfa Beach. If you don't fancy that, you could walk to (the much closer) Conwy Castle and start the route there.

HIRE & LESSONS

There are currently no companies renting paddleboard equipment or offering lessons in this area so come prepared.

WHERE TO STAY & EAT

On Bangor Road in Conwy, The Archway (☏ 01492 592458) does excellent fish and chips. However, to avoid their single-use plastic cutlery be sure to take your own spork! For accommodation options, see ⟨ visitllandudno.org.uk.

TITBITS

Although the route is relatively straightforward, it's not really suited to beginners. As tides can move quickly and waters can get choppy (particularly in breezy conditions), you need some experience and confidence.

36 MANCUNIAN SECRETS

DISCOVER WORSLEY'S UNDERGROUND WATERWAYS, HIDDEN AWAY OFF THE BRIDGEWATER CANAL

WHERE	Bridgewater Canal, Greater Manchester
STATS	↔ 16.5km (10¼ miles) one-way ⓘ
START	Monton Lighthouse, Ellesmere Park ⚲ SJ763995
FINISH	Plank Lane Lift Bridge, Pennington ⚲ SJ631996

Paddling in Britain isn't always about scouting for wildlife, marvelling at mountains or battling against the swells of the open sea. There is a lot to be said for gently paddling through leafy suburbs, sleepy villages and bustling towns to get a real sense of life in Britain. The suggested route along the Bridgewater Canal (⌗ bridgewatercanal.co.uk) offers a cracking way to get under the

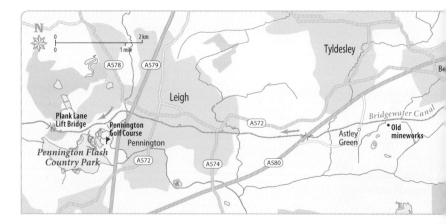

↑ The Packet House in Worsley, where you would have bought your ticket for local boats in the 18th century. (April Wilson/D)

skin of a humdinging metropolitan area, in this case Greater Manchester. Here you will encounter people going about their daily routines along the towpath and admire the parkland that swathes the periphery of this conurbation. Of course, like any major city, you should expect the usual graffiti-clad bridges and waterways tragically rich in rubbish. But look beyond this to some seriously impressive history along the Bridgewater that is definitely worthy of a little admiration.

PADDLE THIS WAY

Launch from the banks of the Bridgewater Canal at the foot of one of its strangest landmarks: the white-and-red Monton Lighthouse. Perhaps unsurprisingly, it is believed to be the only lighthouse on the British network of inland waterways so make sure you get a snap of it! Admittedly, other than this striped building, the start of this route is not the most romantic of settings. But it does offer fascinating glimpses of city life along the waterways.

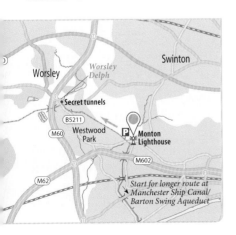

From here the scenery opens out a little, with parkland on the left (west) and a golf course on the right (east) accompanying you until you reach the leafy suburb of Worsley, which is

reportedly being considered for World Heritage Site status thanks to its rich, varied and 'secret' history. You soon reach a small fork in the canal. The route continues left (west), passing under the roadbridge (known as Alphabet Bridge). This is close to Worsley's oldest surviving building, constructed in 1725 as a nailmakers. Rather than continuing, why not investigate some of those local secrets?

To do so, paddle right (northeast) towards a small arch that introduces Worsley Delph. Sandstone was once quarried here – including to build the Bridgewater Canal. Today, this section of the canal is bricked off but you can easily explore it by foot. Two tunnels lead to 74km (46 miles) of underground canals and, up the steps and across the road, to the Delph itself.

Look closely to observe marks made by quarrymen's picks and chisels as well as shot holes, which were filled with explosives to blast away large chunks of rock. Spare a thought for those quarrymen. Working conditions here were abysmal as men laboured by candlelight on their knees. Moreover, this was a job fraught with danger: gas explosions and tunnel collapses were not uncommon.

↑ The Barton Swing Aqueduct can be seen on a longer paddle (see *Titbits*, opposite). (Jakub Trunec/S)

Passing under the M60, paddle a temporary goodbye to the industrial and urbanised segment of this route and welcome the rural landscape that flanks the canal towards Boothstown, where your first landmark is a marina. Pass the old mine workings of Astley Green to your left (south) then paddle beneath the A580, a dual carriageway. You then re-enter concrete-dominated land at Leigh. As the town ebbs away, the green spaces of Pennington Golf Course then Pennington Flash Country Park open out to your left.

In summer, this area is full of dog-walkers and other people enjoying some comparatively fresh air. You are now within sight of the finishing 'line' of Plank Lane Lift Bridge. Before you remove your vessel from the water, notice the latter's colour. Ochre (an earthy pigment containing ferric oxide) from old coalmines still leaks into the canal, giving the water a harmless, rusty-orange tint. Pull out by the Lift Bridge and dial a taxi to take you back to the start.

GETTING THERE

Leave the M60 at junction 13 and take the B5229 south then east through Westwood Park. Just after you cross the canal, turn left into a car park (SJ763996). Walk south to launch from the lighthouse at SJ763995. Nearest train station is Patricroft (which you can reach from Manchester Oxford Road station). From here walk 1km (⅔ mile) north to the launch point.

HIRE & LESSONS

Unfortunately, there are currently no providers renting paddleboard equipment or offering lessons on the Bridgewater Canal. A market opportunity for the taking, if you are an entrepreneurial sort?

WHERE TO STAY & EAT

Try The Old Boathouse (oldboathouseastley.co.uk) at Astley Green. Refurbished in rustic style, there's even a wooden pontoon where you can moor your board before refuelling. Should you need accommodation, Novotel Manchester West is close to the canal near Worsley (tinyurl.com/novo-manc).

TITBITS

Fancy a longer paddle? If so, start the route southeast of Barton-upon-Irwell. At Redclyffe Road (SJ767976), you can launch on to the Manchester Ship Canal from its southern bank. Paddle right (east) towards the Barton Swing Aqueduct, built in 1894 and still operational today. Like Lune Aqueduct on the Lancaster Canal (page 180), this is one of the architectural wonders of Britain's waterways. Hang around long enough and you may see it swing open to allow ships, laden with cargo, in and out of Manchester Docks. Then head north along the canal for 2km (1¼ miles) to Monton Lighthouse, where the route proper commences. Note that while licences permit canoes and kayaks on this route, paddleboards are not currently afforded the same rights owing to health and safety concerns.

37 SKIP TO SALTAIRE

PADDLE THE LEEDS & LIVERPOOL CANAL
THROUGH THE DALES TO A WORLD HERITAGE SITE

WHERE	Leeds and Liverpool Canal, North/West Yorkshire
STATS	↔ 25km (15½ miles) one-way ②
START	Belmont Wharf, Skipton ♀ SD987516
FINISH	Salt's Mill, Saltaire ♀ SE142381

Not for nothing is Skipton known as the 'Gateway to the Dales'. This lively market town provides a fantastic starting point for adventures in this beautiful part of God's Own County, Yorkshire. Saltaire is absolutely worth a visit in its own right. The 19th-century village takes the name of Sir Titus Salt, an industrialist and philanthropist who constructed the settlement to provide homes for workers at his world-leading textile business, housed in Salt's Mill.

Sitting proudly on the banks of the River Aire, Saltaire is now a World Heritage Site. The mill has been developed to include an art gallery that showcases the world's largest collection of work by artist David Hockney as well as housing several eateries. What finer way to visit both Skipton and Saltaire than to paddle between the two along the Leeds–Liverpool Canal as it passes through tranquil woodland, productive farmland, local villages and – most remarkably of all – Britain's steepest flight of locks, Five Rise Locks at Bingley?

↑ Hirst Mill in Saltaire operated as a corn mill in the 17th century. (Steve Morris/D)

PADDLE THIS WAY

From Belmont Wharf in the centre of Skipton, paddle past the market-town bustle and out of the canal basin, heading south under Gallows Bridge, along the Leeds–Liverpool Canal. Soon you leave the market town behind and emerge into farmland that accompanies you to the village of Low Bradley, 4.5km (2¾ miles) from the start. A little further along, on the left (east) bank of the canal, you will pass a memorial to seven Polish airmen who were killed when their Wellington bomber crashed nearby in 1943.

Continuing, you pass the villages of Farnhill and Kildwick before the canal swings east and views open up along Airedale (the valley of the River Aire) towards the town of Silsden (which lies straight ahead of you). Silsden's most bizarre claim to fame is that a resident grew what was once the world's biggest ever onion. On either side of the valley, green fields strain upwards to the moorland tops, the southern side above Keighley being the 19th-century home of the Brontë family. The uplands themselves provided inspiration for the bleak literary creations of *Wuthering Heights* and *Wildfell Hall*.

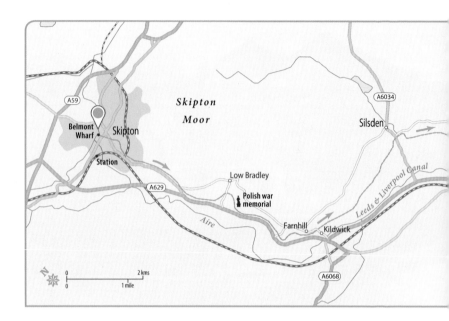

After Silsden, a quiet stretch of canal runs for about 1km (⅔ mile) before entering a wooded section, with Alder Carr Wood and Low Wood nature reserve on your left (east) and Keighley Golf Club on your right (west). Keep an eye out for the kingfishers that zip along this stretch, which becomes increasingly urbanised as you pass the outskirts of Keighley and traverse Riddlesden.

After 7km (4⅓ miles), you will reach the famous, Grade-1-listed Five Rise Locks at Bingley. This feat of 18th-century engineering is Britain's steepest flight of locks, descending 18m over 100m of water. Two of the lock gates are the tallest in the country. To fortify yourself before this portage and the Three Rise Locks further on, it may be wise to call in at the Five Rise Locks Café.

Having passed Damart Mill (perhaps pausing in to purchase some new thermals), leave Bingley southeast. A quieter stretch of canal now leads to The Fisherman's Inn. Just beyond this, cross the River Aire on an aqueduct and pass through Hirst Wood. Here the canal runs parallel to the River Aire and if you look down left (north), you may see rowers from the local club. Keep alert and you may even spot another kingfisher.

You're on the home straight now. With a picturesque cricket pitch in Roberts Park to your left (north), between canal and river, you reach the World Heritage Site of Saltaire. Leave the river at Salt's Mill. It's a long paddle and will take well into the evening to complete, especially if you plan to stop for lunch en route. The good news is that there's no need to paddle back. From Saltaire, there is a direct train back up the valley to Skipton, taking 20 minutes.

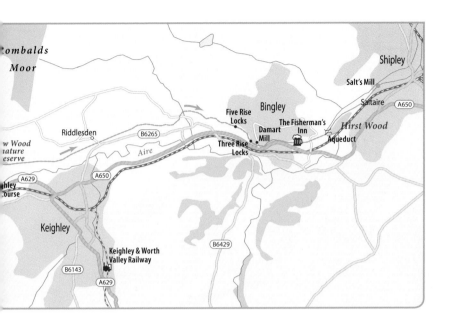

GETTING THERE

Skipton is easily reached from all directions via a variety of A roads. Use Cavendish Street, Coach Street or Waller Hill car parks, then walk to Belmont Wharf canal basin. The starting point is also an easy walk from Skipton train station.

HIRE & LESSONS

You'll need to bring everything with you, as there's nowhere to rent equipment along this stretch.

WHEN TO GO

Longer summer days with light evenings will make this relatively long-distance paddle more relaxing, and allow time to take in the beautiful Yorkshire surroundings.

WHERE TO STAY & EAT

In Skipton, Herriot's Hotel (⌂ herriotsforleisure.co.uk) offers accommodation and the excellent Rhubarb restaurant. Fine traditional pubs in town, serving local ales and fantastic food, include The Narrowboat (⌂ tinyurl.com/narrowboat-skipton) and The Woolly Sheep Inn (⌂ woollysheepinn.co.uk); the latter also offers lodging. Five Rise Locks Café (⌂ fiveriselockscafe.co.uk) serves breakfasts, baked potatoes and toasted sandwiches. The Fisherman's Inn (☎ 01274 510479) offers canalside food. In Saltaire, The Boathouse Inn (⌂ theboathouseinn.co.uk) serves the local Saltaire Blonde beer. Salt's Diner in Salt's Mill (⌂ saltsmill.org.uk/#diner) offers a good range of food options, with menus designed by David Hockney!

38 WATERWAY JUNGLE

EXPLORE THE LOST WORLD OF THE LANCASTER CANAL

WHERE	Lancaster Canal, Lancashire/Cumbria
STATS	←→ 14km (8¾ miles) one-way ①
START	Cinderbarrow Lane, Burton-in-Kendal ♀ SD519752
FINISH	Stainton ♀ SD520854

Built early in the 19th century, the Lancaster Canal rapidly flourished as a waterway for transporting coal and limestone through northwest England. The canal spent its first 190 years in isolation from the rest of England's network of artificial waterways until it was finally hooked up in 2002, when Stainton, a few miles south of Kendal, became connected with Preston.

Competition from adjacent landscapes – the Silverdale coast, Morecambe Bay, the Forest of Bowland and the Wyre – means that the Lancaster Canal is often all-but-forgotten, and certainly overlooked. For avid paddlers, however, this is no great loss. To the contrary, indeed, for it means that even on the busiest stretches, on the most glorious of days, and in high summer, there is no waterborne traffic. This leaves the paddler free to be awed by a full 360° of rustic British countryside – grazing pastures and expansive fields – in absolute peace. Beyond admiring the landscapes, the real clincher for paddlers is that this waterway boasts 66km (41 miles) of – wait for it – lock-free cruising! This is the longest 'clear' run of any English canal – an accolade that holds great appeal for the many of us who crave smooth, faff-free paddling. Even better, you won't encounter a single boat.

For this you should thank the Highways Agency (or its predecessor, half-a-century ago). When the M6 was constructed, the most northerly section of the canal – the stretch featured in this chapter, which locals call the 'Northern Reaches' – was chopped up, rendering it inaccessible to boats. For paddlers with a sense of adventure, this is thus a route to savour. Today, this section of canal is largely untouched. In fact, some parts are so remote and forgotten that the footpath is overgrown with bushes, and shrubbery spills on to the canal giving it ever so slightly the feel of an unexplored Amazonian side channel. A little piece of the jungle in Lancashire? Let's go!

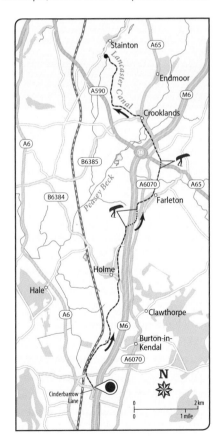

PADDLE THIS WAY

Launch from the canal banks parallel with Cinderbarrow Lane and the M6, just southwest of Burton-in-Kendal.

← When you reach Farleton, you are more than halfway through your journey along the Lancaster Canal. (Philip Birtwistle/S)

Proximity to the motorway means that paddling is quite noisy initially but it does quieten off as canal and road part company. Regale in the jungle-like environment before the landscape begins to open up. The sweeping countryside thus revealed stands in vigorous contrast to the narrowness of the canal. You'll draw level with the village of Burton-in-Kendal (east of the M6) and then pass Holme (to the west), where stone bridges add to the waterway's charm.

About 1.5km (1 mile) after Holme, you reach a dead end, which signals a need to portage. Follow the underpass east beneath the M6, then rejoin the canal. If the sun is shining take time to notice the shapes and shade created by trees overhanging the water. Beyond the village of Farleton (to your right/east), you will need to portage under the A65. Then continue through landscape with ever more buildings until you reach the village of Crooklands.

This is where the 'stand up' part of SUP can be appreciated. Stand tall to fully take in the vistas – something that sadly is not possible with canoeing or kayaking. In the distance you'll get a glimmer of Lake District fells and peaks horseshoeing the canal. Take a moment to stand back and give free rein to your senses. 'Hear' the stillness of the countryside, and savour the magnificent rural views as you continue on the final leg of this wonderful journey.

↑ The 'Northern Reaches' of the Lancaster Canal are so secluded as to be a lost world. (Russell Howard)

The last few kilometres are nothing less than beautiful. Wildlife is abundant (although note that the mute swans can be rather aggressive, particularly during the breeding season). And while the luxuriant green of the trees and bushes that line the canal could be distracting, they fail to shroud the wider views – instead somehow enhancing them.

The end point of this spectacular paddle, just southwest of the village of Stainton, comes abruptly. A gravel path brings the canal to its final resting place – the northernmost point of England's canal network. It's all a little underwhelming. But at least the journey there more than makes up for it.

GETTING THERE

From the M6 junction 35, take the A601(M) then the A6 north. Turn east on to Tarn Lane (in the direction of Burton-in-Kendal), then go south immediately on to Cinderbarrow Lane. Cross the model-railway line and park in the layby next to the canal and motorway. By public transport, the nearest train station is Lancaster. From that city's bus station, take bus 555 towards Ambleside, Grasmere or Kendal. Get off at Longlands Hotel just before the M6 roadbridge. To get to the start point, you can walk about 2km (1¼ miles), order a taxi or start paddling north from near Tewitfield Marina.

HIRE & LESSONS

No local providers cover this rather remote stretch of canal, so you need to come equipped.

WHEN TO GO

This route is sheltered and unaffected by tides, so any time of year is fine. However, its reasonable length means that it's better to paddle on days with longer daylight hours.

WHERE TO STAY & EAT

Towards the end of the route is Little Acre campsite (☎ 015395 67214) at Crooklands. To reach it, exit left on the towpath, walk through a small gate and the site is directly across the road. In Holme, you could try The Smithy Inn (⌂ smithyinn.co.uk) or stay at Marwin House B&B (⌂ marwinhouse.co.uk).

TITBITS

To experience more of this beautiful canal, why not start further south? If you launch from Lancaster city centre, for example, look out for something rather surprising waiting for you on the bench next to bridge 33. Here you'll find a book and pen inside a little waterproof bag, with a message inviting anyone sitting on the bench to share their reasons for being there. Sift back to June 2016 and you might find a note that I inscribed... Rural views aren't the only thing worth admiring – it also features renowned architecture. Located in the southern reaches of the canal, the Lune Aqueduct was designed by renowned engineer John Rennie and built in 1797. Some 200m long, it transports the canal 16m above the River Lune.

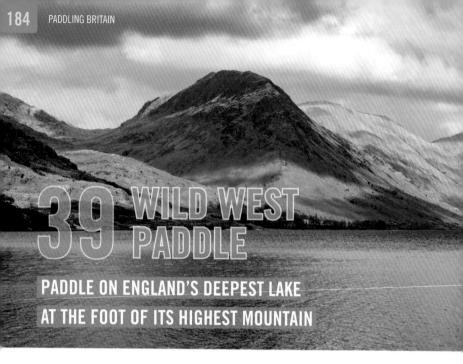

39 WILD WEST PADDLE

PADDLE ON ENGLAND'S DEEPEST LAKE AT THE FOOT OF ITS HIGHEST MOUNTAIN

WHERE	Wast Water, Cumbria
STATS	←→ 10km (6¼ miles) round trip ①
START/FINISH	Northeast corner of Wast Water ♀ NY181070

Huddled in the quiet western fells of the Lake District, Wast Water (or Wastwater) is a world away from the hubbub of Windermere or Derwent Water (page 188) – and thus provides a very different and altogether wilder experience for the paddler. The view along the lake towards the hulking masses of Kirk Fell, Great Gable and Scafell Pike (England's highest mountain, lest you forget) has been voted Britain's favourite, according to a poll conducted by the ITV series *Britain's Favourite View*. How better to appreciate it than from the water on Britain's deepest lake? With England's smallest church in the adjacent hamlet, this truly is a route of superlatives.

PADDLE THIS WAY

From the car park at the northeastern end of Wast Water, follow the path from Brackenclose down to the lake's southern shore by Wasdale Head Hall Farm. Once on the lake, track the southern shore broadly southwestwards. To your left (south), the fell side rears steeply up to the summit at Illgill Head, more than 600m above you.

Halfway along the lake, again to your left, you get a close-up view of the famous Wasdale Screes. This broken hillside of tumbled boulders broods menacingly over the dark water. None of Windermere's gentle rolling hills here; you're in the Wild West (of Cumbria).

↑ Wast Water: today, England's deepest lake is yours for the taking. (Daniel_Kay/S)

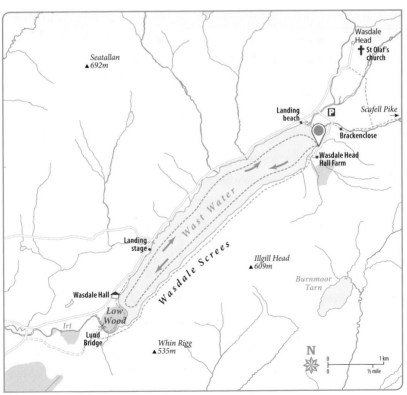

Guarding the southern edge of the Screes is the summit of Whin Rigg (535m). As you reach the southwestern tip of the lake, you come to Low Wood and the mouth of the River Irt. Should you fancy some scenic variation, you can follow the river for 500m (⅓ mile) downstream through the woods to Lund Bridge. Just bear in mind that your return will be upstream, so play within your energy levels.

Back on Wast Water, follow the wooded shore round to the northern edge of the lake. Passing Wasdale Hall youth hostel, you reach a landing stage. Take a breather here and climb ashore to fully appreciate the view southeast across to Wasdale Screes and northeast along the lake to the high fells. Take the obligatory photo before returning to the water. Continue northeast towards Wasdale Head, still flanking the north shore. Here the lake plunges to 79m; its deepest point is 15m below sea level.

Land on the beach at the northernmost corner of the lake and switch to a land-based activity – one where your legs assume primary responsibility for locomotion. Wasdale Head hamlet is a short walk along the valley. Here you'll find the Wasdale Head Inn, renowned as the hangout of the Victorian pioneers of rock-climbing. St Olaf's church is also worth a visit. England's smallest church is said to date from before the Norman Conquest; legend has it that some of the roof beams are from a Viking longboat. Then paddle back the short distance to your launch point to finish.

↑ Canoeing on Wast Water. (kbw-travel/A)

GETTING THERE

Wasdale and Wast Water are a long way from anywhere – but the journey to get there is worth it! Turn off the A595 near Holmrook and head towards Irton and Santon Bridge. From here, follow the country lane towards Nether Wasdale and onwards to the lake. Use the National Trust car park (📍NY182075) at the northeastern corner of the lake. Walk south then southwest to launch near Wasdale Head Hall Farm.

HIRE & LESSONS

Equipment hire is available from Lake District Paddleboarding (🖉lakedistrictpaddleboarding.co.uk) who also offer guided tours and lessons on Wast Water.

WHEN TO GO

The water temperature rarely gets above 10°C, so, for the most comfortable conditions, late summer would be best. That said, a crisp winter's day with snow on the surrounding fells would be magical.

WHERE TO STAY & EAT

The Wasdale Head Inn (🖉wasdale.com) is a veritable institution and no trip to Wast Water would be complete without a visit. As well as food and drink, they have bedrooms, self-catering apartments and a campsite. Wasdale Hall Youth Hostel (🖉yha.org.uk) is right on the water and situated in a beautiful setting.

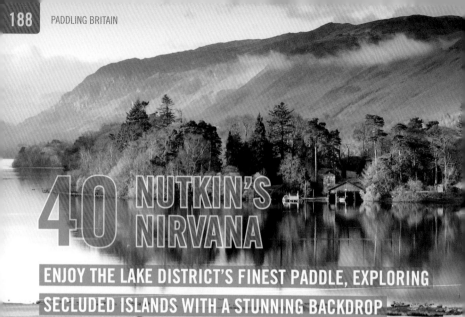

40 NUTKIN'S NIRVANA

ENJOY THE LAKE DISTRICT'S FINEST PADDLE, EXPLORING SECLUDED ISLANDS WITH A STUNNING BACKDROP

WHERE	Derwent Water, Cumbria
STATS	↔ 11km (6¾ miles) round trip ①
START/FINISH	Lake Road, Keswick ♀ NY263227

Surrounded by snow-capped fells, Derwent Water is a place of considerable beauty and justifiably one of best-loved waters of the Lake District. The hills serve a practical purpose too – windbreaks for paddlers in this routinely breezy region. The wood-lined lake stretches for 4.6km (2¾ miles) and is dotted with 13 choice islands, all demanding exploration by intrepid paddlers. A scenic and exciting paddle is assured.

What's more, Derwent Water is an important area for wildlife – a Site of Special Scientific Interest. Although the chances of seeing one are negligible, the lake is home to perhaps Britain's rarest fish, the vendace, which is an ice age relic. While paddling or resting on the lake shores, you may spot red squirrel, otter or wading bird such as snipe and common sandpiper. Report any red squirrels you see to a group called Red Squirrels Northern England (⌀ rsne.org.uk/sightings), which monitors the species's status.

Should you encounter one of the bushy-tailed, bright-eyed, tuft-eared tree-climbers, there's an outside chance that one of its ancestors may have inspired a famous children's book. Rumour has it that Beatrix Potter was staying by Derwent Water when she wrote *The Tale of Squirrel Nutkin*.

PADDLE THIS WAY

Launch from the landing stage on Lake Road, just south of Keswick on the eastern shore of Derwent Water. Before starting to navigate clockwise, get your bearings. Look south – the direction you will travel – and locate Derwent Isle around 300m ahead. Paddle between this and the eastern shoreline, making for a small headland

↑ One of the first things you see after launching is this secret entrance to Derwent Isle. (stocker1970/S)

(Friar's Crag), which protrudes into the lake a further 400m ahead. You may be able to see the Ruskin Monument on top. This honours art critic and social thinker John Ruskin who declared the view from this point as one of Europe's most beautiful. Friar's Crag is believed to have served as the departure point for monks on pilgrimage to St Herbert's Island as early as the 7th century.

Some 300m further on, you come to Lord's Island. Keep west of the island as the east is designated a no-paddle zone. An 18th-century manor house hidden within the island's trees is open a few times a year – so plan ahead should you wish to visit. Access is via a pier on the island's west shore.

Continue tracing the east shoreline in a southerly direction for 800m (½ mile) until you reach Calfclose Bay. Notice the 100-year-old stone, split in two, which

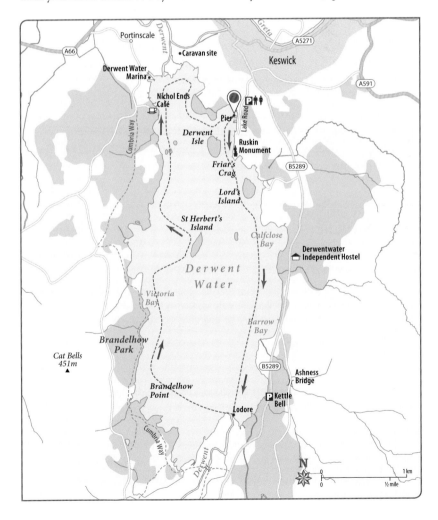

sits in isolation on the shingle shoreline. Made of boulder and volcanic rock from nearby Borrowdale, the carving marks the centenary of the National Trust's role in caring for special places in England and Wales.

Continue 1.5km (1 mile) south past Barrow Bay and on to Lodore, which lies where the southern shore of Derwent Water curves west. Observe the small opening where the River Derwent feeds the lake. If conditions are benign, perhaps travel 800m (½ mile) upstream to view the Chinese-style bridge and boardwalk, located where the river and lake converge.

GETTING THERE

Derwent Water (⊘ tinyurl.com/derwent-water) is immediately southwest of Keswick, which lies at the junction of the A66 and A591. From central Keswick, take the B5289 south then turn right (southwest) on to Lake Road. Park in Lakeside car park then walk southwest to the landing stage to launch. Nearest train station is Penrith, from where it is a 40-minute bus journey to Keswick (on the X5). Realistically, driving or hiring a car makes more sense. After all, even if you have an inflatable board or craft, you're likely to travel with a fair bit of kit.

HIRE & LESSONS

Equipment – including canoes, kayaks and stand-up paddleboards – can be hired from various providers based around the lake, including Keswick Canoe & Bushcraft (⊘ keswickcanoeandbushcraft.co.uk).

WHEN TO GO

My favourite time to paddle on Derwent Water is late afternoon and early evening, when you can watch the sun dip behind the Grasmoor group of fells above the western shore, illuminating the sky with mesmerising hues of red, pink and purple.

↑ Kayaking between Derwent Water's 13 islands can be tough work, so go with a friend! (Iain Frazer/S)

Back on Derwent Water, Great Bay is a no-paddle zone, so head northwest to Brandelhow Park, then paddle north. Notice the steep incline of Cat Bells in the distance. Although the hill's height is fairly modest compared with many round here – just 451m – it's a popular haunt for hikers looking for panoramic views over Derwent Water. Paddling for 2km (1¼ miles), you pass Brandelhow Point, Brandelhow Park and the landing stage at Victoria Bay until you draw parallel with St Herbert's Island to your right.

Covering 4–5ha, St Herbert's is the largest of Derwent Water's islands. It is also the most revered. The name is a respectful nod to St Herbert who sought hermitage on the island that now takes his name. After his death the island became a place of pilgrimage. Today paddlers are able to moor up on its banks and explore. In fact, if you rummage among the undergrowth you will find St Herbert's cell. which is still discernible today.

Another 700m (½ mile) ahead, a smattering of small islands comes clearly into view. Paddle through them until you reach the village of Portinscale at the northwesternmost point. This is where the rivers Greta and Derwent converge. It's also the location for Derwent Water Marina; in summer, this is a popular launch spot for boaters, so beware of novices.

Crawl along the shore keeping an eye out for a flicker of mammalian movement that might signify a red squirrel. As you pass the caravan site in the lake's northeast corner, in Keswick, you will curve back round south and reach your start point.

WHERE TO STAY & EAT

Wild camping is a possibility (page 11). If you fancy a proper bed, an inexpensive option is Derwentwater Independent Hostel (⌀ derwentwater.org). In Portinscale, Nichol End Café lies close to a jetty where you can moor your board.

TITBITS

Note that the launch point in Keswick can get busy at peak season so an alternative would be to try Kettlewell car park, located on the southeastern shores, and then to follow the same circular route. You may be surprised that I am not featuring Windermere in this book, given that it is one of the world's best-known lakes. Surrounded by rugged landscapes and unpredictable conditions, it epitomises everything I adore about the British countryside and is undeniably always a place for adventure. Accordingly, it would be criminal not to give Windermere a gentle nod. However, it's simply not my personal favourite paddle in the Lakes. In summer, Windermere is just too busy with tourists, which is why I advocate exploring its quieter sisters – Derwent Water, Ullswater (page 192) and Wast Water (page 184).

→ Derwent Water is a key location for red squirrel. (Menno Schaefer/S)

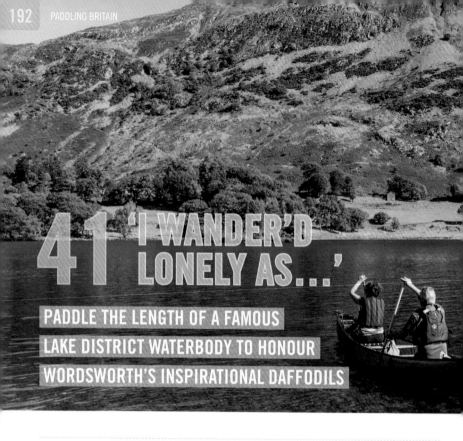

41 'I WANDER'D LONELY AS...'

PADDLE THE LENGTH OF A FAMOUS LAKE DISTRICT WATERBODY TO HONOUR WORDSWORTH'S INSPIRATIONAL DAFFODILS

WHERE	Ullswater, Cumbria
STATS	↔ 12km (7½ miles) one-way ⓘ
START	Lakeland Boat Hire, Pooley Bridge ⦿ NY468241
FINISH	Glenridding ⦿ NY390169

For pretty much anyone who loves the outdoors, the Lake District needs little introduction as a Mecca for adventure. On land some of the country's best hiking trails and climbing routes enthral numerous visitors. But let's pause a moment – to reflect on the region's name. The Lake District doesn't take its name from craggy mountains, which implies that one of the very best ways to explore this stunning part of England is from the water.

The slow pace of life in the Lake District lends itself perfectly to paddling. Glide gently across the water surface at strolling pace, encumbered with nothing but a blade to propel you and let breathtaking vistas envelop you. Magnificent rugged hills rise from the shores of the long, narrow lake of Ullswater – England's third-highest mountain, Helvellyn, is accessed from the village of Glenridding at the waterbody's southern tip. The lake's beauty is enhanced by any seasonal touch, whether spring flowers to a dusting of snow, the reflections of puffy clouds or the early-morning mist introducing a flat-calm day.

Ullswater has plenty of fascinating geological and historical features too, each of which add interest to an already special paddle. There are quiet islands perfect for wild camping. There are beautiful, secluded

↑ The Lake District may be famed for its mountains, but its name honours waterbodies such as Ullswater. (SS)

bays. And, along Ullswater's inaccessible eastern shoreline, there are cliffs and even a headland. There's even the added bonus of a chance to spot one of England's rarest mammals around the water.

Then there's Ullswater's cultural resonance. It is said that William Wordsworth was inspired to pen his famous poem *Daffodils* ('I wander'd lonely as a cloud...') after an early-spring visit to Ullswater – the time when parts of the shoreline are covered in vibrant yellow hues of the familiar flower. But you need not restrict your visit to spring. Every season offers its own particular enchantment. Across autumn, for example, trees lining this sinuous lake evolve shades of crimson and rust-red, mustard-yellow and olive-green.

PADDLE THIS WAY

Ullswater is often paddled from south to north to capitalise on the prevailing southwesterly winds. However, if you plan a return journey this really doesn't matter; the toughness of the paddle will be down to weather conditions on the day. My itinerary travels north to south.

Begin your paddle on the pontoon at Lakeland Boat Hire, on the eastern shore of Ullswater, immediately south of Pooley Bridge, a small village that sits

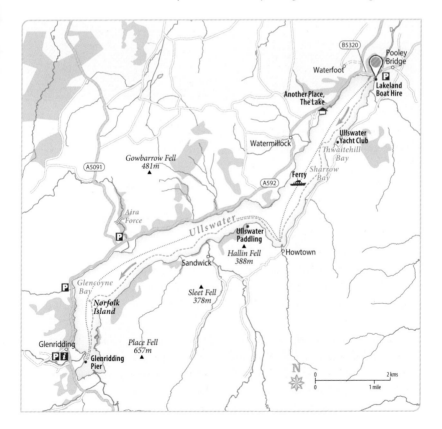

at the lake's northern tip. Red deer often roam the land here. Among abundant birdlife, look out for greylag goose (in flight, distinguished by its pale grey-blue upperwings) and cormorant.

Paddle south, roughly tracing the of the eastern shore for 5km (3 miles) – passing points of interest such as Ullswater Yacht Club, Thwaitehill Bay and Sharrow Bay – until you spot a wooden jetty protruding from the bank. This marks your arrival in the cosy hamlet of Howtown. The Lake District is a fine place to see peregrines and ravens, both of which are often seen above Howtown as they explore the skies over Ullswater. Either sighting would make for a red-letter day. So this is an ideal place to stop for a moment, and give yourself the chance to spot one. If all else fails, there are breathtaking views of the crags of Hallin Fell. Let all the wildness soak in.

Continue following the shoreline southwest for another 7km (4⅓ miles). En route you pass the village of Sandwick on your left (south) and (2km beyond Sandwick) arguably the Lake District's most famous waterfall (to your right, the north). Unfortunately, Aira Force is not visible from the water, but it is within walking distance of the shore, should you wish to paddle across to the opposite

↑ Can there be a boathouse with a finer view than that at Pooley Bridge on Ullswater? (Daniel_Kay/S)

bank and take a look (small charge for non-members of the National Trust; nationaltrust.org.uk/aira-force-and-ullswater). Woodland around Aira Force is also a national stronghold for red squirrel, so peer into the trees for your chance to see this rarity.

On the water continue tracing the dense deciduous woodland along the eastern shore. Where Place Fell swells to your left (south), look towards the strip of land at Glencoyne Bay on the western bank. This is the site of Wordsworth's daffodils; in early spring (when the flowers bloom), you may wish to paddle over, by way of Norfolk Island with its surround views of the lake, to take a look.

By now the lake is running pretty much north–south. Accordingly, you are heading south and the land is starting to encroach to each side and ahead of you. As you pass a small promontory to your right (west), the jetty at Glenridding (and home to a National Park information centre) will cleave into view. Take advantage of this easy place to pull up, and end your paddle. Assuming you have an inflatable board, you can the take the steamer back along the lake. With a hard board, taking the boat will be at the skipper's discretion. Conversely, if you've got enough grit left, why not fill your boots by paddling back?

Wordsworth's daffodils, the flowers at Glencoyne Bay that inspired his famous poem. (SS)

GETTING THERE

Ullswater lies alongside the A592 between Windermere and Penrith, and is accessed southwest of junction 40 of the M6. Pooley Bridge is 1km (⅔ mile) along the B5320, east of the A592 at the northern tip of Ullswater. There are car parks on either side of the roadbridge. Walk south along the lake's eastern shore to reach Lakeland Boat Hire (⚓lakelandboathire.co.uk), where you launch. Nearest train station is Penrith, from where you can take bus 508 to Pooley Bridge.

HIRE & LESSONS

Ullswater Paddleboarding (⚓ullswaterpaddleboarding.co.uk) provides equipment and guided tours. Another Place, The Lake (see *Where to stay & eat*, below) also offers guided paddleboarding and kayaking around Ullswater.

WHERE TO STAY & EAT

Another Place, The Lake (⚓another.place/the-lake/) – yes, that really is its name – is a converted Georgian hotel set in 7ha of grounds, and boasts private access on to Ullswater. Howtown Hotel (⚓howtown-hotel.co.uk) has been owned by the same family for nearly a century: its tearoom serves light lunches and homemade cakes.

TITBITS

Ullswater steamers (⚓ullswater-steamers.co.uk) run daily from Glenridding and tour the lake, calling at various points en route to Pooley Bridge. What more relaxing way to return to your starting point? When you are on the water, however, take care when the steamers pass you, they can create a small swell.

42 THE SCOTTISH RIVIERA

ENJOY FINE VIEWS & A BIRD-FILLED ISLAND
ON THIS CRACKING COASTAL PADDLE

WHERE	Rockcliffe, Dumfries and Galloway
STATS	↔ 5km (3 miles) return ③
START/FINISH	Kippford Quay ♀ NX836553

Rough Island, off Rockcliffe in Dumfries and Galloway, is a bird reserve, its breeding shorebirds being protected by the National Trust for Scotland. When tide allows (and outside the birds' breeding season of May to mid-July, when access is prohibited), you can walk to this island from the mainland across the crooked finger of the Solway Firth. Unsurprisingly, I find there's more excitement in paddling there. What more apt way to see oystercatchers and ringed plovers that breed on the 8ha island than from the water that brings the nutrients that nourish those shorebirds' prey?

The little-known Galloway coastline is often marketed as the 'Scottish Riviera' due to the Gulf Stream-influenced microclimate that complements its rolling scenery. Peppered with sailing villages, the beautiful Rockcliffe coast is also fringed with wildflowers that buzz with butterflies such as ringlet in late summer, while rockpools at low tide demand that adults release their inner child. You'll find lovely views from the petite but perfectly formed summit of The Muckle (120m) between Rockcliffe and Kippford (the latter a gloriously pretty and narrow, linear village). There's even a dose of history, as the old hillfort of the Mote of Mark – brooding atop a rocky cliff – was reputedly the preserve of a Dark Age chieftain.

PADDLE THIS WAY

Launch from the quay in Kippford and enter Urr Water, which merges into Rough Firth before draining southeast into the Solway Firth. Paddle downstream along Urr Water for almost 1km (⅔ mile). As you go, enjoy increasingly varied views. The right shoreline (west) brings an abundance of green – notably trees, shrubs and bushes on a small tidal island (Glen Isle) – while the left (east) is residential, decorated with granite and whitewashed houses and rural businesses.

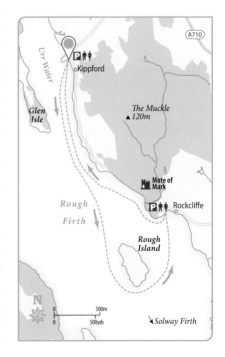

Continue south for almost 1km (⅔ mile) and, to your left (east), you'll approach the bay over which the Mote of Mark has proud purview. While the eastern shoreline has several pristine coves, this one is different. The hillfort, of course, immediately and intrinsically sets it apart. Second,

← The appropriate rocky coast at Rockcliffe on the shores of Rough Firth. (James Johnstone)

↑ The saltmarsh-fringed Urr Water at Kippford. (Creative Nature Media/S)

this sheltered egress from the water is rather enticingly isolated; the only sign of residence is a rather grand granite farmhouse that sits back from the water.

As you pass the Mote of Mark, Rough Island will dominate the view ahead. Paddle to the right (west) to circumnavigate anticlockwise. If access is permitted at the season of your visit, take the time to explore the island, including walking up to the stone cairn at its top. From here you can enjoy peaceful views south to Heston Island and west along the Cumbrian coast. If the weather is clement, you may even spot the peaks of the Lake District – perhaps encouraging you to explore the waterbodies of that region too (pages 184, 188 and 192) .

Worth looking for whatever the weather is little Rough Island's rather quirky surprise: a geocache in the form of a biscuit tin. I won't reveal exactly where the island's 'treasure' is, as this would spoil the surprise of finding it. If you do discover it, read the messages it contains, then use the pens and paper to contribute your own note. Departing the island, head directly east towards the indented shoreline by the village of Rockcliffe. If you fancy a stroll up The Muckle, haul up here. Otherwise head north back to base.

GETTING THERE

From Dumfries (west of the M74), take the A711 to Dalbeattie then the A710 south to Kippford (aka Scaur). Use the car park near the waterfront (⚲ NX837553). The quay is adjacent. Nearest train station is Dumfries, from where you take bus 372 to Sandyhills, then bus 372A to Kippford (⟁ dumgal.gov.uk/timetables).

HIRE & LESSONS

Although several fairly local watersports providers offer lessons and rent kit, none is located on the stretch between Kippford and Rockcliffe so you'll need to bring your own equipment.

WHERE TO STAY & EAT

The Anchor Inn at Kippford (⟁ anchorhotelkippford.co.uk) provides overnight accommodation, food and drink. Its terrace tables overlook the estuary. For a daytime snack or tea try The Ark (⟁ tinyurl.com/kippfordark). Nearest campsite is Castle Point, which offers seaside pitches (⟁ castlepointcc.com; ⏱ Apr–Oct).

TITBITS

The island is accessible by foot at low tide, which is good for walkers but not paddlers. Be mindful of this when planning your journey to avoid having to drag your board across extensive mudflats in order to access a reasonable depth of water.

→ Colourful and exuberant, oystercatchers soon catch the eye on this paddle. (James Lowen)

43 HOLY HISTORIES & CRAFT ALE

EXPLORE THE ARRAN COAST TO EARN YOUR PINT OF THE LOCAL CRAFT BEER

WHERE	Isle of Arran, North Ayrshire
STATS	←→ 7.3km (4½ miles) one-way, plus optional 8km (5 miles) extension from Lamlash to Brodick ③
START	Slipway, Whiting Bay ♀ NS046261
FINISH	Pier, Lamlash ♀ NS029312

Scotland's seventh-largest island, Arran lies off the country's southwest coast, in the Firth of Clyde. First occupied during the Neolithic period, the island is home to many ancient remains. Castles abound, but Giant's Grave, situated on a lofty peak in a forest clearing and overlooking the picturesque departure point for this paddle (Whiting Bay), comprises two chambered tombs. The burial sites were excavated in the early 1900s and were found to contain flint knives, pottery shards and arrowheads, as well as burnt bones.

Whiting Bay harbours a surprising riposte to this context of death. In the bay's northeastern reaches lies Holy Isle, whose spiritual heritage dates to the 6th century. The island currently houses a Tibetan Buddhist retreat. Lama Yeshe Rinpoche runs the Holy Isle Project (⊘ holyisle.org), helping visitors find the *dhammapada* (or, at least, inner peace). Should that not be your cup of tea, perhaps return to Arran itself and check out one (or more) local distillery or brewery.

↑ Holy Isle, home to a Tibetan Buddhist retreat, welcomes visitors. (Riccardo Zambelloni/S)

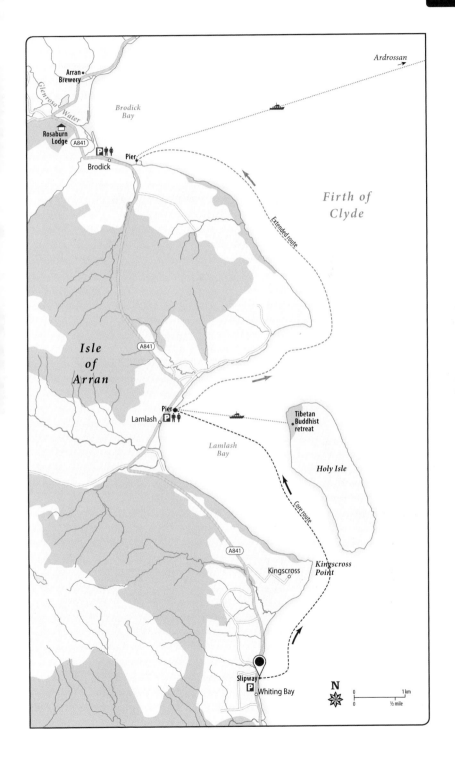

↑ Arran's mountains are best appreciated from the water, here at Brodick Bay. (SS)

PADDLE THIS WAY

Launch from the slipway at Whiting Bay and head left (north) following the coastal road that parallels the sea for 2km (1¼ miles) until you reach the headland of Kingscross Point. Holy Isle, although prominent from Whiting Bay, now reveals itself more vividly to your right (northeast). Start to appreciate its considerable length and, if you intend to land, prepare by contemplating the spirituality of the place.

Paddle northeast a further 0.75km (½ mile) to the small island then navigate 3km (1¾ miles) along the western shore, which runs broadly parallel with Lamlash Bay on Arran. This side of the island is sheltered and therefore provides a gentler paddle. From March to October, visitors are welcome to visit. Seek out the isle's healing spring, 6th-century hermit cave and the remains of a 13th-century monastery. This tiny island bursts at its seams with fascinating history.

Back on the water, continue to the northwestern tip of Holy Isle. Now look due west to see the village of Lamlash on Arran. It's only 1km or so (⅔ mile) away, so potter across. If that is paddle enough for you – and breezy conditions might make the decision a foregone conclusion – stop here then either paddle back to base, keeping tight to the coast to save energy, or catch a taxi/bus back south.

Those with surplus energy might extend the challenge by paddling a further 8km (5 miles) north to Brodick. The town is home to Arran Brewery, which produces craft beers – the perfect reward after a tiring day on the water. It's too far to sensibly paddle straight back to Whiting Bay, so either stay overnight in Brodick before returning or take a taxi back south.

GETTING THERE

To get to Arran, take the MV *Caledonian Isles* from Ardrossan Harbour to Brodick. If you're in your own car, drive south along the A841 to Whiting Bay and use the car park by the slipway/jetty. Details of public transport on Arran are at ⊘ visitarran.com/arran-info/public-transport.

HIRE & LESSONS

SUP Arran (⊘ suparran.com) rents gear and offers lessons.

WHERE TO STAY & EAT

On the outskirts of Brodick, the beautiful Rosaburn Lodge (⊘ rosaburnlodge.co.uk) lies on the banks of Glenrosa Water. Other accommodation options across the Isle of Arran are consolidated on ⊘ visitarran. com/where-to-stay-on-arran. To sample local beers, visit the island's micro-brewery in Brodick (⊘ arranbrewery.co.uk) and take a tour. (For the avoidance of doubt, this recommendation applies whether or not you paddled the extended route…)

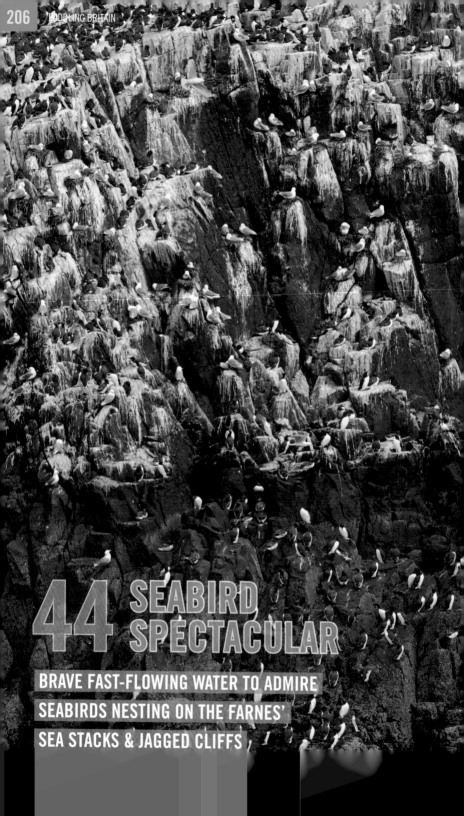

44 SEABIRD SPECTACULAR

**BRAVE FAST-FLOWING WATER TO ADMIRE
SEABIRDS NESTING ON THE FARNES'
SEA STACKS & JAGGED CLIFFS**

WHERE	Farne Islands, Northumberland
STATS	↔ 12km (7½ miles) round trip, plus 10km (6¼ miles) optional extension
	④ but ⑤ for the extension
START/FINISH	Harkess Rocks, Bamburgh ⚲ NU177356

Think of a British island, and Skye or Anglesey or the Isle of Wight might be among the first to come to mind. Skulking off the Northumberland coast, a few miles into the North Sea, the Farne Islands probably wouldn't. But that doesn't render them any less worthy of waterborne exploration. Quite the opposite, in fact.

These chunky, rocky, treeless protrusions are world-famous for the quantity and variety of seabirds that breed here. This coastal citadel houses some 70,000 pairs of birds, their number including Atlantic puffins, guillemots and razorbills. The most dramatic avian encounters, however, are with Arctic terns. Should you inadvertently paddle too close to their nest or young, these feisty 'sea swallows' won't think twice about dive-bombing you – and their sharp bills mean they can even draw blood. Factor in the large colony of Atlantic grey seals, whose curious youngsters adore tailgating paddleboards, and there's never a dull moment around these islands!

As well as being renowned for their wildlife, the Farnes have had two justly celebrated human inhabitants. St Cuthbert – one of northern England's most significant saints – lived as a hermit on the islands from AD676–684. Somewhat closer to our times, Grace Darling was a lighthouse keeper's daughter who courageously saved sailors whose ship was wrecked on the islet of Longstone in 1838.

PADDLE THIS WAY

Launch from Harkess Rocks, 1km (⅔ mile) north of Bamburgh, and start paddling across the open sea. Venturing into the realm of proper waves is unusual in this

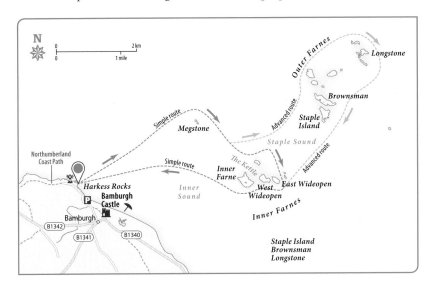

← The seabird city of the Farne Islands, here replete with kittiwakes and guillemots. (David Tipling)

book and is the reason for the grading of this paddle. Head northeast towards the small island of Megstone, an isolated member of the Inner Farnes that lies less than 4km (2½ miles) offshore. Being closer to the mainland, these islands – notably Inner Farne – are the main locus for tourist boats that visit daily from Bamburgh. Given its adjunct location, Megstone is not on their itinerary, and that makes it attractive to the paddler and, particularly, to the Atlantic grey and harbour seals looking to escape human attention.

Paddle round Megstone, keeping it to your right (south), before heading southeast for 1.5km (1 mile) to reach the three other islands that make up the Inner Farnes. The largest of the jagged, igneous stacks is Inner Farne; to its east are West Wideopen and East Wideopen. The trio is connected at low tide. There is easy access to some of the narrow gullies (locally known as 'guts') that schism the islets. Be warned, however, that the thoroughfare that runs between them all, known as The Kettle, has some deceptively fast tidal flow.

As you paddle, see how many species of seabird you can identify. Among the red-billed Arctic terns you may see the larger, black-billed Sandwich tern. Search

↑ Kayakers passing the tern colony and old beacon tower (lighthouse) on Brownsman. (David Forster/A)

too for shags, kittiwakes and various auks, all of which nest on the low rocky cliffs. Eiders may be riding the swell – the drakes white and black, the females mottled brown. Look for three impressive buildings shouldering one another, each with strikingly different functions: a cylindrical, white lighthouse constructed in 1811; Prior Castell's Tower (built around 1500 for the reason of defence); and St Cuthbert's Chapel, which dates to 1369. If you pull ashore, don't count on visiting them all: only the chapel is open to the public. In better news, there is a public toilet on Inner Farne, which may be welcome if you're spending all day paddling.

Once you've fully explored the Inner Farnes, you have a straight choice. You could return to the mainland by heading slightly north of west. Or, if you are both energetic and experienced, you could head northeast, further out to sea, to circumnavigate the cluster of islands that comprise the Outer Farnes. The principal ones are Staple, Brownsman and Longstone.

Be warned, however, that paddling between the Inner and Outer Farnes is a very serious undertaking. It should only be attempted by highly proficient paddlers on calm days.

GETTING THERE

Bamburgh lies northeast of the A1 along either the B1341 or B1342, 28km (17 miles) north of Alnwick. There are two car parks on The Wynding, a no-through road running north from Bamburgh to Harkess Rocks. Walk from here to the beach and launch. Nearest train station is Chathill, but a better bet is to take a train to Berwick-on-Tweed, then catch bus X18 to Bamburgh.

HIRE & LESSONS

If you want to complete this trip you'll need your own equipment. Unfortunately, the most local provider – Kitesurfing Adventure Sports (⊘ kitesurfinglessons.co.uk) – does not cover the Farne Islands (but does offer guided tours around sheltered parts of the coast, if that is of interest).

WHERE TO STAY & EAT

In Bamburgh, The Potted Lobster (⊘ thepottedlobsterbamburgh.co.uk) serves fresh, local seafood every day and although located away from the water's edge, it's close to parking for the launch.

TITBITS

The Farne Islands are owned and managed by the National Trust (⊘ nationaltrust.org.uk/farne-islands). During the seabird breeding season, it is prohibited to land on any island bar Longstone, Staple and Inner Farne. Non-members of the National Trust must make a small payment to land. Camping is prohibited throughout. Back on the mainland, you shouldn't leave without exploring Bamburgh Castle (⊘ bamburghcastle.com). Within its ancient remains, you will discover tales of betrayal, deceit and romance.

45 SOUND OF SILENCE

TASTE ARGYLL'S WILD WATERS ON A PADDLE THAT FLIRTS WITH THE SOUND OF JURA

WHERE	Loch Craignish, Argyll and Bute
STATS	←→ 3+km (1¾ miles) round trip ③–④
START/FINISH	Bagh Dùn Mhuilig, Kirkton ♀ NM780019

The Sound of Jura sits quietly tucked away between the Isle of Jura – home of a famous whisky and a cottage where George Orwell wrote the novel *Nineteen Eighty-Four* – and the mainland of Argyll and Bute. This remote area offers wild and dramatic landscape synonymous with the very best of Scotland.

Loch Craignish is a sea loch that feeds into the northern stretch of the Sound of Jura. From the moment you arrive, you will feel immersed in the rawness and liberating silence of the surroundings. Where the shores are not lined with jagged boulders and rocks, they are indented by tiny sandy bays or draped with dense woodland. And that's just the immediate vicinity. The backdrop features the peaks of sugar-coated mountains standing steep and proud, and even their intervening troughs serve as a constant reminder of your ardent travels to reach this rugged location. This body of water, particularly in its southern section, is laden with skerries. These seem to have a magnetic appeal for wildlife. You shouldn't need to spend

↑ Extend your day by paddling northeast along Loch Craignish to the village of Ardfern. (Christina Bollen/A)

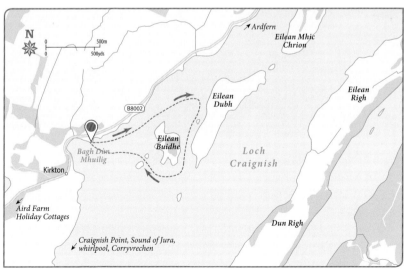

long on the water to stand a good chance of garnering some interest from nearby otters or seals, both mammals being curious about new visitors. White-tailed eagles and great northern divers are among the birds that you may see; the former swooping overhead and the latter hulking on the sea, rather like a sturdy cormorant.

One thing you hopefully won't see on Loch Craignish, however, is a boat chase. Wind the clock back to 1963, however, and you might have done – for this loch was the location for James Bond's waterborne pursuit in the film *From Russia with Love*.

↑ Weather can quickly turn inclement on the coast, so it pays to dress cautiously (page 14). (Lizzie Carr)

PADDLE THIS WAY

Launch from the western shore of Loch Craignish, just north of the bay of Bagh Dùn Mhuilig, which marks the entrance to the hamlet of Kirkton. Looking south and east, you will see a few little islands dotted around. The closest, Eilean Buidhe, is just 300m from the launch point – so head there and start exploring. Haul up on the shores of Eilean Buidhe and investigate the terrain by foot. Then mosey east and repeat the adventure on the neighbouring larger island of Eilean Dubh. There's no right or wrong way of doing this; just potter and follow your whim.

If you have more time then extend your route beyond the one mapped, by paddling 3km (2 miles) northeast up Loch Craignish. Opposite the northern tip of another island, Eilean Mhic Chrion, is the small village of Ardfern. Here you will find small boats moored along the shores, a local pub in which to relax and a marina around which to stroll before heading back aboard.

Alternatively, head southwest along Loch Craignish towards the Sound of Jura itself. If you paddle far enough, you may just hear the roaring of the notorious Gulf of Corryvreckan, the world's third-largest tidal whirlpool, which lies 7km (4⅓ miles) northwest of the headland of Craignish Point. This is too far to paddle – and best admired from a commercial boat anyway.

GETTING THERE

Private transport is the easiest way to reach this paddle. Take the A816 south from Oban, turning off on the B8002 to reach Ardfern, a distance of 40km (25 miles). From Ardfern, continue southwest along the B8002 for 4km (2½ miles) until you reach Bagh Dùn Mhuilig, just north of Kirkton. Park carefully by the roadside and launch. Nearest train station is Oban, from where you can take bus 3 or 423 as far as Ardfern.

HIRE & LESSONS

You can rent kayaks from Sea Kayak Oban (⬧ seakayakoban.com), which is based in Oban. If you want to paddleboard, however, you will require your own equipment.

WHERE TO STAY & EAT

Self-catering is available at Aird Farm Holiday Cottages (⬧ craignishholidays.co.uk). For something quirkier, try Ardfern Tipis (⬧ ardferntipis.co.uk) as a 'native' alternative to traditional camping. Northeast of Ardfern, The Gallery of Lorne Inn (⬧ galleyoflorne.co.uk) offers food, drink and accommodation.

TITBITS

The east end of the Sound of Jura holds some serious dangers, notably strong tidal currents. Only head southwest out of the safety of Loch Craignish if you are an experienced paddler – even for the experienced, the Corryvreckan whirlpools can be perilous.

46 REPEL THE VIKINGS

PATROL THE EXTENSIVE SANDS OF LUNAN BAY, A 12TH-CENTURY CASTLE TO YOUR BACK

WHERE	Lunan Bay, Angus
STATS	↔ 7km (4⅓ miles) return ②
START/FINISH	Lunan Bay 📍NO691511

The coastline of Angus boasts mile after mile of picturesque coastline, much of it without peer anywhere in Scotland. Yet it is the innocuous little bay of Lunan that somehow grabs one's attention. Invaded by the Vikings in the 10th century, this secluded strand fronts the North Sea. It continues to receive plenty of visitors – though today's arrivals are somewhat less malign in intent. So what is the pull?

Perhaps it is the expansive sand dunes, framed by sandstone cliffs sprayed with candy-pink thrift. Or maybe the lure is the varied wildlife Lunan Bay attracts – from common scoter (a seaduck that bobs offshore) to shorebirds such as ringed plover (with its matching orange bill and legs). (Keep an eye out too for common bottlenose dolphins, which occasionally plough watery furrows along this coast.) Or it could even be the crumbling remains of Red Castle built in the 12th century to repel further Viking invasions. This sandstone fort sits at the mouth of a small river, Lunan Water, that drains into Lunan Bay. Or it could be a mix of them all. Whatever the reason, the 3km (2 miles) of sandy bay oozes magnificence and demands to be paddled.

PADDLE THIS WAY

From Lunan village car park, walk roughly east down to the shoreline and prepare to launch. Leave the shores of Lunan Bay and paddle north for 3km (2 miles) until you reach a rocky promontory, cave and arch at Boddin Point. Here you can explore the combination rockpools and 17th-century limestone kilns that make this spot unique. On the Point's more sheltered western side there is a small concrete slipway, which enables you to egress and explore. That said, evidence of recent erosion suggests that paddling close to the base of the cliffs might require a hard hat so be careful.

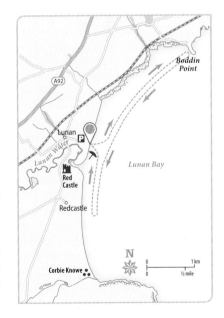

As you turn back south towards the other end of the bay, admire the foreboding ruins of Red Castle. This was built originally in the late 12th century for King William the Lion to ward off Viking invasions. Once you're done return to the golden beach just north of the channel of Lunan Water.

← There's no shortage of launch points on Lunan Bay. (SS)

The remains of the 12th-century Red Castle are a striking landmark on the fringes of Lunan Bay. (David Robertson/A)

GETTING THERE

Lunan Bay is east of the A92 between Arbroath and Montrose. Leave the A92 at Inverkeilor and take minor roads northeast to Lunan. Use the village car park, then walk southeast to the shore. Nearest train station is Montrose, from where you are best off taking a taxi to Lunan. Realistically, private transport is more practical.

HIRE & LESSONS

Paddle Surf Scotland (⌂ paddlesurfscotland.com) provides lessons, hire and equipment.

WHERE TO STAY & EAT

Lunan Farms (⌂ http://lunanfarms.co.uk) offer a diner, campsite, bunkhouse and self-catering chalet. All are conveniently located, tucked away behind Lunan Bay.

TITBITS

On the shores of Lunan Bay, you may spot nets that are strung to poles and dug into the sand. This area is one of the last few locations in the UK where traditional nets are used to catch salmon as tides recede.

47 HIGHLAND FLING

PADDLE AROUND RUGGED ISLANDS AS YOU EXPLORE THE FRINGES OF THE ARDNAMURCHAN PENINSULA

WHERE	Loch Sunart, Highland
STATS	←→ 22km (13⅔ miles) round-trip ⏳ one long day ③
START/FINISH	Laga Bay, Loch Sunart ⚲ NM632609

There isn't a single loch in Scotland – freshwater or salt – that would make for a disappointing paddle. This made it tough to whittle down my longlist into this book's final selection. Loch Sunart, however, was a shoo-in from the get-go. And for several reasons. It is the longest sea loch in the Highlands. It is surrounded by majestic mountain scenery. And yet it is far enough off the tourist trail to be captivatingly tranquil.

Moreover, Sunart has a colourful past. Roughly halfway along the loch between Strontian (in the east) and Ardnamurchan Point (in the west), lie the islands of Oronsay and Carna. The latter belonged to the kingdom of Dalriada until invaded by Vikings in the 8th century. Four centuries on, it became part of the Norse–Gaelic dynasty.

The best-known residents of Loch Sunart's sheltered bays, shingle beaches and secret inlets are harbour porpoises, common seals and otters. Along the shoreline, grey herons hunch and oystercatchers roam. Among the mosaic of oak woodland, coniferous plantations, heath and grassland that surround Sunart, you can often spot red deer browsing. And don't forget to look up to the skies as there's every chance a golden or white-tailed eagle will be circling above.

PADDLE THIS WAY

Launch from the slipway at Laga Bay and head east, hugging Loch Sunart's northern shoreline. After 1.5km (1 mile) you will reach a rocky islet accessible

↑ Keep an eye out for otters on Loch Sunart's seaweed-strewn shoreline. (John Dixon)

from land only at low tide. There you will see the Iron Age hillfort of Dùn Ghallain, which means 'Fort of the Storms'. Local legend holds that the fort's ruined ramparts guarded the bodies of a local chieftain and the beautiful but low-born maiden whose affections he craved. His mother, distressed by the affair, used magic to transform the girl into a swan that the chief unwittingly shot and killed – only for it to resume the form of his lover in its dying moments. Overwhelmed with grief, he killed himself. For this reason, swans are absent from Loch Sunart.

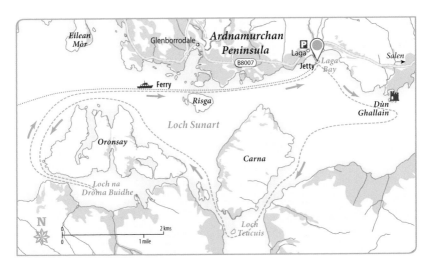

From Dùn Ghallain, turn a full 180° to paddle west back the way you came, heading towards the Atlantic along the Ardnamurchan Peninsula. Directly ahead, after around 2.5km (1½ miles), lies Carna. Rising to 169m, the island excites with its colourful mix of purple heather on moorland, green forest, heady ridges and shingle beaches. See if you can spot all three of Carna's houses as you follow the island's eastern curve for 3.5km (2¼ miles) towards the south shore. Eventually you pass through the narrows to reach the entrance to Loch Teacuis. Gritty sand beaches here are good for a pit stop, but they also offer opportunities to enjoy to look for marine life including otters, seals and porpoises as well as birds of prey.

Leave Teacuis northwest, via another set of narrows, to run along the west of Carna for just over 1km (⅔ mile). Almost immediately, you come across the north shore of the tidal island of Oronsay on your left. This is exposed at low tide and accessible from land by a causeway, but submerged at high tide. If time and tide are on your side (see *Titbits*, page 221), follow Oronsay's northern shore around to Loch na Droma Buidhe, a small sea loch into which you can paddle. Otherwise, set your sights north to Eilean Mòr, an island that protrudes from Loch Sunart's north shore.

Like other parts of Loch Sunart, this uninhabited tidal island is notable for flame shell, a small saltwater clam with vibrantly orange tentacles that would

↑ Preparing for a big day of kayaking around the island of Carna and beyond. (Karl Bungey/Otter Adventures)

seem more in keeping with tropical reefs. Flame shells are tricky to find as they live on the seabed in 'nests' made from stone and rocks, below the low-tide mark and at depths of 5–25m. That said, the tentacles make them easy to identify!

Finish this circular route by paddling back eastwards along Sunart's north shore, past Glenborrodale village. Absorb the views on both south and north shores. The lush undergrowth of the foreground rises into the more dramatic mountains, cloaked in greys and browns. Keeping the islet of Risga to your south, return to 'base' at Laga Bay.

GETTING THERE

Laga is on the B8007, 9km (5½ miles) west of Salen. Use the hamlet's roadside car park and cross the road to Laga Bay jetty. If coming by public transport, you could take a train or bus to Fort William (if you're coming from London, consider taking the Caledonian Sleeper), then hop on Shiel Bus 506 (⊘ shielbuses.co.uk) towards Kilchoan. Alternatively you could hire a car from Fort William and drive the 60km (40 miles) to Laga.

HIRE & LESSONS

Arisaig Sea Kayak Centre (⊘ arisaigseakayakcentre.co.uk) offers sea-kayaking options. You can rent equipment from and take trips with Otter Adventures (⊘ otter-adventures.co.uk).

WHEN TO GO

The summer months offer calmer waters and less windy conditions, which are key factors for this route.

WHERE TO STAY & EAT

For an overview of local accommodation and eating options, see ⊘ ardnamurchan.com. On the shore of Loch Sunart, Resipole Farm (⊘ resipole.co.uk) offers paddling packages as well as overnight accommodation including camping pitches.

TITBITS

Be careful! Sea lochs are tidal and the water can be very fast flowing. Check the tides: it is best to paddle Loch Sunart at mid- to high water to get through the narrows and into Loch Teacuis. Moreover, it takes only a few minutes for weather and water conditions to change rapidly. Accordingly, less experienced paddlers should plan carefully, and, if in doubt, book the services of a qualified guide. Should you wish to explore further afield from Loch Sunart, you'll be heading away from shelter into more unpredictable open water which leads to the major islands of Mull, Coll or Tiree. This is a serious undertaking and not for a beginner.

↑ Eyes on the skies! There could be a golden eagle up there. (Vladimir Kogan Michael/S)

48 LOCH LOVE

EXPLORE A TRANQUIL LOCH BEFORE RECLINING ON BRITAIN'S LONGEST FRESHWATER BEACH

WHERE	Loch Laggan, Highland
STATS	↔ 5km (3 miles) round trip ②
START/FINISH	Bridge over River Pattack by A86 ♀ NN539897

Open-access laws in Scotland make the country a playground for watersports. This journey provides unbridled fun, combining a beautiful paddle on a freshwater loch with lounging on a beach – with the complement of a walk to stunning waterfalls. The slender form of Loch Laggan, between Newtonmore and Spean Bridge, measures 11km (7 miles) from tip to 'toe'. It lays claim to harbouring Britain's largest freshwater beach – a highly suitable resting spot after a paddle.

PADDLE THIS WAY

From the pull-in on the A86, walk carefully down the steep slope to the water's edge. It's a cumbersome start to a paddle but worth it. You quickly reach the pebbly

↑ Loch Laggan: calm despite the imminent storm. (Philip Bird LRPS CPAGB/S)

banks of the narrow River Pattack, from where you launch. Head west down the River Pattack and you soon enter Loch Laggan at its northeasternmost point.

Gaze left and a beautiful, pale sandy beach, stretching away southwards, will dominate your view. Reputedly Britain's largest freshwater beach (presumably there are folk who measure such things), it will doubtless be devoid of people and thus perfect for lolling and picnicking. But not yet. The reward will come at the end of your paddle, not the start.

So head west, past a jetty, keeping parallel with the northern bank of

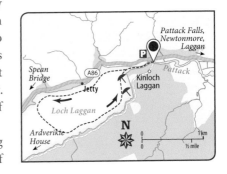

Loch Laggan – with the snow-capped peak of Stob Coire Easain in the distance to the southwest. You may spy a few cars speeding along the A86, which runs just beyond the shoreline. But otherwise you are free to regale in the stillness. Enjoy the serenity that comes with paddling an inland waterbody. No crashing waves, no sloshing water – just you and your board, in your element. You are free of strictures, free to do what you want, when and how.

Accordingly, there's no particularly fixed route for this paddle. Go where whim and wind take you. At some point cross southeast to the southern shore of the loch. Deciduous trees cloak the banks here. You may glimpse the odd walker or mountain-biker. But they do not disturb the tranquillity. Were you to head southwest, you would reach Ardverikie House – the fictional Glenbogle in the TV series *Monarch of the Glen* – on the south shore. Assuming you fancy a shorter paddle, keep the sylvan shroud to your right (south) and head northeast towards the record-breaking strand. Here you can relax, recuperate and replenish energy levels until it's time to paddle back into the River Pattack and return to your vehicle.

GETTING THERE

The A86 from Spean Bridge to Newtonmore runs along the north side of Loch Laggan. Approaching from the east, just before the loch opens up, a bridge to your left (south) crosses the River Pattack. Park in the roadside pull-in here (NN539897). Walk to the river to launch. Nearest train station is Newtonmore, from where you could conceivably take a taxi to the launch point. But, to be frank, private transport is more practical.

HIRE & LESSONS

Wilderness SUP (wildernesssup.co) provides guided tours around Scotland and can organise a visit to Loch Laggan. They also supply equipment and kit.

WHERE TO STAY & EAT

The nearest places to eat are near Laggan, northeast of the loch: Laggan Wolftrax Café (lagganforest. com/laggan-wolftrax-cafe.asp) and Caoldair Coffee and Craft Shop (01528 544231). Alternatively, it's a beautiful destination for a picnic.

TITBITS

Lined with fern-smothered crags, Pattack Falls are hidden away in Scots pine forest east of Loch Laggan. Sadly it is too tough to get there by paddling up the bubbling River Pattack. Instead, follow footpaths to reach the cascades. If you're brave enough, go for a dip: sit on the rocks to feel the water massaging your back. A truly special sensation.

↑ As you paddle your eye keeps returning to the distant snow-capped peak of Stob Coire Easain. (Lizzie Carr)

49 SKYE'S THE LIMIT

PADDLE TO THE INGRESS OF SCOTLAND'S MOST-FAMOUS SINGLE MALT DISTILLERY

WHERE	Loch Harport, Isle of Skye, Highland
STATS	↔ 7km (4¼ miles) round trip ②
START/FINISH	Jetty northwest of Talisker Distillery car park ⚲ NG376321

The dominant context for Skye is the sea. This is unsurprising, given that Skye is an island – Britain's second largest, no less. Tucked away in the northwest of Scotland, it provides the gateway to the Hebrides archipelago. On Skye's west coast, Loch Harport is a sea loch that flows northwest into the enormous, bay-like Loch Bracadale. Ostensibly Harport isn't the most remarkable of the island's lochs; there are plenty worthy of exploration. But Harport does lay claim to a unique accolade – one that sets it apart from its 'rivals'. On its otherwise innocuous southern shores lies the original distillery of Talisker, one of Scotland's most famous single malts. Some 40,000 people flock through the distillery's doors each year. So what better way to enjoy a trip to Skye than sampling the intense notes of its finest malt after a day exploring its dramatic coastline? SUP then sup!

Flanked by the muted greys and browns of the Cuillin Mountains, Loch Harport is almost as well regarded for its fishing as for its whisky. Fishermen here have been known to land quite some diversity of catches – rays, dogfish, dab, flounder, cod and conger – which inspire you to have a bash from your board. If you do so, why not target the pollock and mackerel that congregate close to the surface on calm days – then cook it up on a barbecue later?

PADDLE THIS WAY

Use the Talisker Distillery car park (⚲ NG377319) in Carbost, then walk 300m northwest to launch from the floating pontoon. Then, simply, explore. I don't suggest following a fixed 'route' as such. In part that's because there isn't an obvious one. But it's also partly because this is a part of the world that – unless you are

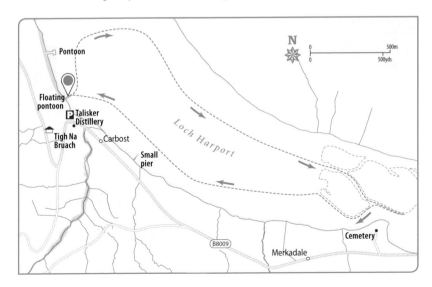

← Carbost village enjoys marvellous views of Loch Harport. (stocker1970/S)

local – is away from everything, which is reason enough to dispense with formality, to take the time and space to relax, and to indulge in nature in its purest form.

If, however, you fancy taking the route I took on my visit, then read on (and see the map, where my paddle is marked). As you launch, paddle northwest along the shoreline for about 700m (½ mile), past a small pontoon on your left, before crossing northeast towards the northern shore. Trace the latter upstream (southeast) for 4km (2½ miles) until you reach the head of the loch. The backdrop of layers of hills and mountains around the loch brings new depths to the paddle. Small mounds in the foreground are backed by mightier (and often snow-capped) mountains in the distance.

↑ Remote, rugged and relaxing: a paddle in Talisker waters is hard to beat. (SS)

Curve around the southern shoreline and make your way back down the south side of the loch. This means that you again proceed roughly parallel with the littoral, initially past a cemetery and the village of Merkadale. Around 2km (1¼ miles) further on, you return to the launch point… but not before you reach the USP of this paddle. We kept the best for the end!

About 350m after you pass a short pier on the left, pause at a modest outflow of water that runs under a small bridge that sits on the lochside. Here is the entrance to the Talisker Distillery. Pull up on to the bank and enjoy a tour before paddling (or walking; it's only 300m back to the car park). Please resist the temptation to taste the malt; drink-paddling is as dangerous as drink-driving. We have kept the best for the end!

GETTING THERE

The Talisker Distillery (⟨⟩ tinyurl.com/visit-talisker) is roughly midway along the Isle of Skye, on the west coast. Turn off the A863 on to the B8009, and follow this for about 4.5km (2¾ miles) to Carbost. There is free parking here. Public transport is sparse in this area and while bus 608 runs from Portree to Fiskavaig (close to the distillery), having a car on the island gives a lot more flexibility (and there's plenty to explore!). That said, Fort William 170km (106 miles) away is fairly well served by rail, including the famous Caledonian Sleeper, which runs from London Paddington each evening. So you could take public transport to Fort William then hire a vehicle for the last leg.

HIRE & LESSONS

Explore Highland (⟨⟩ explorehighland.com/sup-skye/) offers guided tours of the waters around the island. Sea to Skye Experience (⟨⟩ seatoskyeexperience.co.uk/sea-kayaking/) offers sea-kayaking trips around Skye.

WHEN TO GO

The milder weather of summer makes this the obvious season to choose. But there's something to be said for an autumn or winter adventure. Provided you are not doing the driving, a cold paddle also provides the perfect justification to warm up with a wee post-paddle dram.

WHERE TO STAY & EAT

Caora Dhubh (⟨⟩ www.caoradhubh.com) is a small independent coffee shop on the shores of Loch Harport, close to the distillery entrance. It focuses on locally sourced, ethical products with environmental considerations at their core. I was delighted to walk in here for a slice of brownie after a paddle to discover that all the shop's coffee cups are completely biodegradable. If you are paddling on Skye pop in and show your support! For an overview of where to eat or stay on Skye, see ⟨⟩ isleofskye.com. Particular accommodation options close to the distillery include The Old Inn and Waterfront Bunkhouse (⟨⟩ theoldinnskye.co.uk) and Tigh Na Bruach (⟨⟩ bedbreakfastskye.co.uk), which provides views over Loch Harport and the Cuillins.

50 DESERT ISLAND DELIGHTS

GET AWAY FROM IT ALL WITH A COASTAL PADDLE WHERE YOUR ONLY COMPANY IS RABBITS

WHERE	Rabbit Islands, Highland
STATS	←→ 9km (5⅔ miles) round trip ④
START/FINISH	Talmine Bay ♀ NC586627

Scotland is famous for its islands. You will certainly have heard of – and probably visited – Skye, Shetland and Orkney. You've probably heard of Mull, Harris and Tiree too. But are you privy to Scotland's best-kept insular secret? Hidden away in the far north of Scotland, dotted off the coast of the historic county of Sutherland, are the Rabbit Islands.

The 'Rabbits' comprise three small islands and are locally known as Eileanan nan Gall, which means 'island of the strangers'. The reason for the islands' English name requires little guesswork. Sandy soil enables one particular animal to thrive here: rabbits. Their burrows are very much in evidence.

↑ Paddle across Tongue Bay to reach the Rabbit Islands, hovering on the horizon. (SS)

If you count yourself as intrepid and want to get away from it all, a paddle to and around these uninhabited islands is a must. Jagged rock formations are interspersed with secluded bays of fine white sand. And there's not a person in sight. Desert island delights, indeed.

PADDLE THIS WAY

Launch from the sands of Talmine Beach, a tiny indent on the western shore of Tongue Bay. To your left (north) small sailing boats pepper the water close to the slipway and an old shipwreck dominates the west corner of the beach. Look straight ahead (east) to see your destination – the Rabbit Islands – hovering just about 1.5km (1 mile) from the shoreline.

Paddle due east across Talmine Bay to reach the nearest (most southerly) of the island trio. The small sandy shore that comes into view invites exploration. Climb the steep, grassy slope and head for the top of the island to enjoy spectacular views across the sea and towards the two more northerly islands. On a clear day,

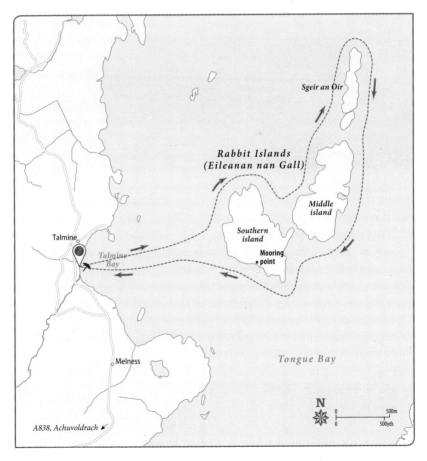

distant mountains command your attention to the south. Return to the water and head north along the island's west coast before making a break eastwards for 500m (⅓ mile) to the middle island.

Continue to trace this island's rocky western edge until you enter clear water. Ahead of you is the slender form of the third island, Sgeir an Oir, which demands attention due to its considerable height (43m at its peak). Head along its western coast, then loop round over its northern tip to start coming back south.

Continue along the eastern coast of the middle island, then sweep southwest towards the southern island. At this point, a small sandy bay materialises to your right (north). At low tide, the sandy spit even unites the two islands. Moor here and walk to the flat top of the southern island. Here you will have no problem finding its special inhabitants – rabbits! Once you're done, the lush greenness beyond Talmine Beach may be calling your name. If so, paddle back west to the mainland. Or, if you can't bear leaving the solitude, why not wild-camp? Just check conditions before you commit to an overnighter on these largely unsheltered rocks.

↑ Feel free to vary your route to take in natural delights such as this beach near Talmine Bay. (SS)

GETTING THERE

Even getting to somewhere this remote makes for a proper expedition. Leave the A838 at Achuvoldrach and take the minor road north to Talmine. Park in a beachside layby, then launch. Nearest train station is Inverness and the nearest airport is Wick, but you will need to hire a car and drive the remaining (not inconsiderable) distance.

HIRE & LESSONS

Paddle Surf Scotland (⊘ paddlesurfscotland.com) provides equipment and can help plan adventures to the Rabbit Islands.

WHERE TO STAY & EAT

If you are considering wild camping on the Rabbit Islands, read page 11 first. You can stay, eat and drink at The Craggan Hotel (⊘ thecraggan.co.uk) in Melness.

EPILOGUE

Ahead of me – indeed, all around me – is nothing but blue. Water and sky merge, disorienting me. It dawns on me that I have completely lost sight of land. For the previous hour, Dover's white cliffs had served as my bodyguard. Now the geological giants had vanished. Leaving just my board, my paddle and me.

After my 2016 expedition along England's waterways, designed to call out the havoc our addiction to plastic is wreaking on our rivers and canals, it felt like a natural next step to cross the English Channel by paddleboard. Natural, but not straightforward.

I finally left the Sussex coast early in the morning of 18 May 2017. It had taken nearly three weeks to get the nod that the inclement weather would break long enough for me to become the first woman to paddle solo between England and France. Conditions wouldn't be perfect – but if you wait for everything in life to be perfect you'll be waiting a long time. At least, that was what I told myself to enter a mindset suitable for the challenge that lay ahead. So I chanced it.

Rising early, I arrived at Rye Harbour to be greeted by a glassily flat sea and clear blue skies. A gentle northerly wind would propel me towards France. Such amenable conditions eased the nerves that had beset me for several weeks. Crashing waves, huge swells and gusty winds had featured in my nightmares. I had woken up to the opposite.

For the first 8km (5 miles) I could look back and see the British coastline. I appreciated watching familiar landmarks shrink, as they demonstrated that I was making progress. But when I arrived at the world's busiest shipping lane, the British coastline had evaporated. I was unequivocally at sea.

Paddling deliberately away from land goes against everything paddlers are taught. If you can't see the sea floor, they say, you're too far from shore. And if you can't see land at all – then you're in real trouble.

I'd equipped myself in every practical sense – hydration packs to keep my fluids up, carbohydrate gels to prevent cramping, neoprene boots to avoid hypothermia if I fell in. And I had trained hard to deal with the anticipated physical challenges but it transpired that there was one issue that I completely overlooked. Seasickness.

Some 3km (2 miles) into the container thoroughfare, I was feeling awful. For the first time, I questioned my ability to complete the cross-Channel challenge. Mindset is as important as physical strength and stamina and my confidence was falling – fast. I lay back on my board contemplating the rest of the journey – I was barely two-fifths of the way through – and loosened my buoyancy aid. Almost immediately, I felt better. Sitting up, I took a deep breath and ploughed on. I had to finish this.

My physical resurgence enabled me to reflect on the sister purpose of my crossing. This wasn't merely an adventure. I was counting pieces of plastic and taking water samples to test for microplastics and microbeads – tiny plastic fragments that harm marine wildlife and have now entered the human food chain, causing all sorts of health implications.

By now, I had been paddling for over 5 hours. I had found my rhythm, controlled my seasickness and was looking forward to completing the challenge.

It was, nevertheless, a relief to get a first glimpse of land. Visibility was dwindling and the weather deteriorating – so seeing France provided an invaluable fillip.

With 6km (4 miles) to go, the worsening conditions were making things really tough. My calves were cramping and the change in wind speed and direction was fatiguing me rapidly, forcing me to paddle against a strong crosswind. Seeing the twin towers of Boulogne Harbour meant that I had halved the remaining distance. The landmark granted me access to energy sources I didn't know I had. Digging deeper, I pushed on towards the shoreline.

Reaching the finishing point was surreal. It was quite enough to get my head around paddleboarding between two countries. But to know that I was the first woman to achieve this particular cross-Channel feat was almost overwhelming.

And then? Well, my emotions were mixed. Elation for sure, and relief too. But when a challenge finishes, there is also a sense of emptiness. You've trained for months and made sacrifices in other aspects of your life. Then, in just one day, it's all over. Done. Gone. Achieved. Vanished.

Until the next time…

↑ Lizzie paddling out into the English Channel. (Neil Irwin)

FURTHER INFORMATION

BOOKS

Canoe & Kayak Map of Britain Peter Knowles, Rivers Publishing UK 2014

Canoeing: The Essential Skills & Safety Andrew Westwood, Heliconia Press 2012

Stand Up Paddle Instruction Book Mitch Powers, CreateSpace Independent Publishing Platform 2013

Stand Up Paddling: Flatwater to Surf and Rivers Rob Casey, Mountaineers Books 2011

Walk on Water: A Guide to Flat Water Stand Up Paddling Vie Binga & Tim Ganley, CreateSpace Independent Publishing Platform 2016

WEBSITES

British Canoeing ⌀ britishcanoeing.org.uk (including for licensing)

British Stand Up Paddle Association ⌀ bsupa.org.uk

Broads Authority ⌀ broads-authority.gov.uk (for licensing in Norfolk Broads)

Canal and River Trust ⌀ canalrivertrust.org.uk (including for licensing)

Environment Agency ⌀ tinyurl.com/e-agency (for licensing)

Magic Seaweed ⌀ https://magicseaweed.com (for weather and sea conditions)

Met Office ⌀ metoffice.gov.uk (for overall weather)

Plastic Patrol ⌀ plasticpatrol.co.uk

Scottish Canals ⌀ scottishcanals.co.uk (including for licensing)

Wind Guru ⌀ windguru.com (for winds)

YR ⌀ yr.no/?spr=eng (useful for weather on coastal paddles)

APPS

There are smartphone apps for Magic Seaweed, Met Office and Wind Guru (see *Websites* above). Two other apps that I recommend are: Tides Planner, which gives information on tides; and Paddle Logger, which you can use to map your routes and take inspiration from other paddlers.

INDEX

Something different for the weekend

Whether wild camping or wildlife-watching, let us help you make the most of your weekends.

Bradt

Available to buy in all good bookshops or on www.bradtguides.com

f BradtTravelGuides 🐦 @BradtGuides 📷 @bradtguides P bradtguides

First edition published October 2018
Bradt Travel Guides Ltd
IDC House, The Vale, Chalfont St Peter, Bucks SL9 9RZ, England
www.bradtguides.com
Print edition published in the USA by The Globe Pequot Press Inc,
PO Box 480, Guilford, Connecticut 06437-0480

Text copyright © 2018 Lizzie Carr
Maps copyright © 2018 Bradt Travel Guides Ltd. Includes map data © OpenStreetMap contributors
& contains OS data © Crown copyright and database right (2018)
Photographs copyright © 2018 Individual photographers (see below)
Contributing Editor: James Lowen
Project Managers: Anna Moores, Laura Pidgley and Anne-Marie McLeman
Cover research and design: Pepi Bluck, Perfect Picture

The author and publisher have made every effort to ensure the accuracy of the information in this
book at the time of going to press. However, they cannot accept any responsibility for any loss, injury
or inconvenience resulting from the use of information contained in this guide. All rights reserved.
No part of this publication may be reproduced, stored in a retrieval system, or transmitted in any
form or by any means, electronic, mechanical, photocopying, recording or otherwise without the
prior consent of the publisher.

ISBN: 978 1 78477 603 9 (print)
e-ISBN: 978 1 78477 554 4 (e-pub)
e-ISBN: 978 178477 455 4 (mobi)

British Library Cataloguing in Publication Data
A catalogue record for this book is available from the British Library

Photographs
All photographs © individual photographers and local businesses credited beside images and also those
from picture libraries/tourist boards, credited as follows: Alamy Stock Photos (/A); Dreamstime.com (/D);
Getty Images (/G); Shutterstock.com (/S); South Downs National Park Authority (/SDNPA); SuperStock (SS)

Front cover Top image: Paddleboarding, Isle of Wight (sOulsurfing - Jason Swain/G);
Bottom image: A kayaker's-eye view of a river paddle (Peter Cade/G)
Title page Lizzie paddling Loch Laggan (Lizzie Carr)
Author photo © Owen Tomkins Photography
Back cover Lizzie taking a well-earned breather on the Oxford Canal (Neil Irwin)

Maps David McCutcheon FBCart.S & Daniella Levin

Typeset and designed by Josse Pickard
Production managed by Jellyfish Print Solutions; printed in India
Digital conversion by www.dataworks.co.in